FAITH AT WORK

Published by Relational Mission
Jubilee Family Centre, Norwich Road, Aylsham, Norfolk, NR11 6JG, UK
www.relationalmission.org

ISBN 978-0-9954778-4-1

Acknowledgements

Scripture quotations taken from the Holy Bible, New International Version Anglicised Copyright © 1979, 1984, 2011 Biblica
Used by permission of Hodder & Stoughton Ltd, an Hachette UK company
All rights reserved.
'NIV' is a registered trademark of Biblica UK trademark number 1448790.

A catalogue record of this book is available from the British Library.
Cover Design and typesetting by Andrew Khatouli

FAITH AT WORK

Workplace testimonies of young Christian professionals
from Revelation Church, London

Compiled by James Slater
and Published under Relational Mission.

Acknowledgements

To the twenty-four people that have input to this book: thank you for your openness and honesty in sharing your story so that it might be an encouragement to others.

To Andrew Khatouli for designing the cover, James Welburn for proofreading and Daniel Hayter for providing a theological review: thank you for all your practical help towards making this book possible.

To those who are a part of Revelation Church: thank you for your commitment to "one anothering" one another, particularly for the way you have cared for and challenged each other in relation to your jobs and workplaces.

To the ten speakers who have helped us with our Faith at Work breakfast series: thank you for contributing to the journey we have been on as a church to help us work out how to be effective Christians in our workplaces.

Foreword

When we planted Revelation Church, one of our fears was that we might become just a ghettoised "holy huddle", tucked away in a little room somewhere, happily singing our songs but disconnected from the world around us. This book is confirmation and a great encouragement that this has not happened.

This really is a beautiful book. As I read it, I was close to tears a number of times. Having the privilege of helping to shepherd the congregation that wrote this book, I know these people and so the stories are very real to me.

I was struck by the depth of character displayed by the contributors: their conviction to hold Christ as supreme, their faith-inspired courage, their humble willingness to embrace the pain of tough life-lessons and their determination to be changed into the image of Jesus rather than trying to get Him to change into theirs! This is the body of Christ, the hands and feet of Jesus, getting up on Monday mornings and applying what they have heard and fed on the day before.

As they cram onto tubes and trains, risk their lives in cycle lanes, and hunt out "office space" in coffee shops, they love the unlovely, create beautiful things, honour difficult managers, dream heavenly dreams, manage big accounts, zoom in on impossible detail, believe the best, refuse to give up on people, stay awake in boring meetings, invent solutions to terrible problems and wisely navigate corrupt systems. These people, the body of Christ, are breathtaking.

As ever, Jesus is showing Himself faithful and true through very normal lives that are devoted to Him and willing to truly trust Him. Jesus is showing that He cares about our workplaces: our colleagues, clients and customers. Jesus is showing that He has a plan for both our individual lives and the whole cosmos. Jesus is showing that as we all look to Him, He can both hold it all and weave it all together into something that makes the most beautiful sense. Through these faithful lives, a true picture of the glorious Christ is painted. This book gives us a window into a small part of our contribution to what Jesus is doing through His people, otherwise known as the church, around the world.

I wholeheartedly recommend this book and would like to take the opportunity to thank the team that has served us so well through Faith at Work at Revelation Church. You have done a great job.

Thank you.

Stefan Liston
One of the pastors at Revelation Church, London

Introduction

Work and the Church

It is often said, 'the church is not a business.'

Although the above statement is correct, I have found that this phrase can subtly distort people's understanding of God's view of work because it can be heard as if church is "good" and business, or even work, is "bad".

By contrast, we know that God highly values His people's contribution to their workplaces. It was in fact the first way that Adam worshipped God: by working and keeping all that God had created (see Genesis 2:15).

At Revelation Church, London we have resolved to communicate that work is good, godly and a wonderful opportunity to worship God.

We have sought to remind people that God values work and we encourage our church to make a God-inspired contribution in their workplaces as if it is worship to God, because it is (see Colossians 3:23).

In 2015, and as a result of this conviction, we set up a series of bi-monthly workplace breakfasts. We called this series Faith at Work. This was set up to encourage, equip and connect the many professionals that we had in our church.

Those at Revelation Church really took to this initiative and many benefitted from the speakers (seasoned professionals from a variety of industries) that came to join us for each of the breakfasts.

Work and Christians

It is a wonderful privilege for me (as one of the leaders) to watch on as these messages and the thoughts of our speakers are taking root in people's lives and as they have started to affect the way people are working.

This book is a celebration of all God has done in the lives of those that have been impacted by the message that work is important to God.

In the pages that follow you will have the opportunity to read a number of workplace God stories from around London as some of our young professionals share their experiences of trying to live out God's will for them in their workplace and honour Him through their work.

As an inner-London church we are predominantly made up of young adults (many just starting out in the world of work). Young though we may be, we are full of faith and seeking God for His plans and purposes and for the way we should conduct ourselves at work each day.

I pray that you enjoy reading these stories and that you too are encouraged to make a God-inspired contribution in your workplace as if it is worship to God, because it is.

How to read this book

You will notice that there are two different contents pages. This is because there are two different ways to read this book.

The first way to read this book is by topic. There are seven subject areas, each with a number of associated testimonies. These include:

- Work and finding meaning
- Work and ambition
- Work and worship
- Work and following God's leading
- Work and church/mission
- Work and family
- Work and trusting God

The second way to read this book is by industry or discipline. All the writers are young and have therefore been working for less than ten years but their experience spans a multitude of areas. These include:

- Medicine
- Business and finance
- Media and arts
- Not-for-profit
- Public sector
- Start-ups
- Sole trader/freelance
- Education

You could work through these testimonies in one go or you might choose to work through these in your individual quiet times with God (i.e. one per day) or with those you meet to do accountability.

Either way you might like to take each testimony and consider (1) in what way the testimony may be similar to yours; (2) what you might learn from the writer; and, as a result, (3) what God is saying to you about how He wants you to glorify Him through the workplace opportunities He has given you.

Now it is over to you! Pick your route through this book, then turn over and enjoy.

Contents
Route 1: By topic

Work and finding meaning

Work and ambition

Work and worship

Work and following God's leading

Work and church/mission

Work and family

Work and trusting in God

Contents
Route 2: By occupation

Medicine

Business and finance

Media and arts

Not-for-profit

Public sector

Start-ups

Sole trader/freelance

Education

Work and
finding meaning

To do, to change and to be changed

Occupation: Management Consultant

Having graduated from university, I took up a position as a management consultant in London. The City – the "big smoke" – I thought it was the place to be! I was to work for one of the biggest global consulting firms. I had made it. I had become a "city boy" and I could not wait to pound the pavements of London in my crisp white shirts, sharp new ties and polished shoes!

However, I soon found that the world was not my oyster after all. Instead I was the oyster, and a little one at that, out of my depth and about to be caught (or found out). I was so unprepared for what was required of me. I soon found that city life was not all it was cut out to be.

I began to experience the result of the fall and God's curse on work (see Genesis 3). I was caught between the monotony of staring at my screen all day and the stress of finding my feet in work that I knew little or nothing about. So much for the crisp shirts and new ties; they counted for nothing!

I began to think, 'Do I even care?'
I began to think, 'I just do not want to be here.'
I began to think, 'I do not belong here.'

However, the biggest question I had, as a passionate young Christian, was whether my contribution to society and to work had any bearing on eternity.

18

Does God really have any interest in management consulting? Does God care about my work, my spreadsheets and my day-to-day?

What ensued was a period of serious reflection and soul searching. If I was to continue with the work I was doing I had to be clear on my work mission. I had to be clear on why I was working and how (if at all) it honoured God.

Through much prayer and reflection I summarised my work mission statement as follows: to do, to change and to be changed.

To do

I developed the first part of this statement, "to do," by saying that I am following God's call to man (before the fall) to be fruitful, fill and subdue the earth (see Genesis 1:28). Adam's first job was to go into the garden to 'work it and keep it' it (see Genesis 2:15). I want to use the talents that God has given me (see Matthew 25:14-30), achieve the good works God has created for me to do (see Ephesians 2:10), and bless others (see Romans 12:8) as I work as if working for the Lord (see Colossians 3:23).

I realised that God's expectations on me for work are simple. I am simply required to do something. Just something! Anything! And yes, I know that does not sound very spiritual but it is incredibly honouring.

I was in danger, as many are, of spending years trying to work out the specifics of what work God was calling me to – expecting to find the perfect fit and my dream job. I agree that God does call people to specific things but this is not the experience of the overwhelming majority. Management consulting is not my dream job but it is a good job, a good fit for my skills and abilities and I enjoy it. Most of all though, I am contributing to God's world, worshipping Him through it and putting my God-given talents to good use.

To change

I have developed the second part of this statement, "to change," by saying that work provides further opportunity to pursue social justice (see Micah 6:8), to provide for my family (see 1 Timothy 5:8) and for future generations (see Proverbs 13:22). Work provides opportunity to meet those who do not know Christ, and to love them by serving them and telling them about Jesus (see Matthew 28:16-20). The workplace provides so many opportunities to have an impact on the world that God has created and to co-labour with

19

do I agree w/ this? I guess it's the fundamental expectation

the first step though I'd probably say 'do something productive'

Him in building His kingdom.

The workplace provides me with the opportunity to meet a lot of people. I remember hearing a London church pastor telling us to "do the maths" on evangelism. He argued that the odds of someone responding to a Christian sharing the gospel are probably fairly predictable. As such the only way to increase the overall odds of people showing interest and/or even responding to the gospel is just simply to meet and speak to more people.

However, I know that I do not need to heap pressure on myself because it is God's work anyway – the Bible says that Jesus will build His church (see Matthew 16:18). We have the privilege of joining with God in that through our work.

To be changed

I have developed the third part of this statement, "to be changed," by saying that the challenges and temptations experienced at work are opportunities to be sanctified and to grow in holiness as I watch the Father (see John 5:18-20 and 1 John 2:15). In addition, my current opportunities provide preparation and training, in anticipation of all that God might do with me in the future.

At work there are many situations where I could compromise my Christian integrity and I regularly have to ask myself questions such as:

- How am I representing myself to others?
- How am I responding when others undermine me?
- How am I talking about others when they are not around?
- How am I making decisions, especially when the right course of action is not clear?

As Christians we live by a very different and high set of standards (see Matthew 5-7). I have realised that it is not always clear what the right direction is and I make many mistakes along the way. However, the process of working this through is hugely important. The Bible describes it as the process of sanctification whereby, through the challenges we face, we work through what it means to honour God and we become more like Christ.

My experience, starting out in management consulting was that "work is not easy" (see Genesis 3:17). However, persevering through that period changed me and I am a much more fruitful worker as a result. I initially really struggled to find meaning and purpose for my work but over time I have realised that the Bible is packed with encouragement and exhortation for those who are wrestling with what being a Christian worker looks like.

Working as a Christian in mental healthcare

Occupation: Doctor training in psychiatry

My work is to help those who are mentally ill. I see people from all walks and ages of life, some who are seeking help and others that are not. One day I may see a twelve year old who is being bullied at school and feeling suicidal and on another day it may be a convicted murderer who is hearing voices commenting on his daily life.

At the core of my work is time spent listening to my patients. The dominant psychiatric approach is the empathic one. This means that I must try to understand a patient's condition from their perspective. I am required to enter their world and describe their suffering. I draw on my medical experience to do this but I also look to Jesus Christ. He became a human and lived in our broken world. He experienced the full extent of human suffering and difficulty (see Hebrews 4:15). This gives me inspiration and strength to draw alongside my patients and to enter their world.

Of course, describing a problem does not solve it, but it is vital so that the correct help can be given to those who need it. I remember a patient from my first month working in a psychiatric hospital. She was not physically disabled but her daily functioning had deteriorated to the extent that she was living in a care home and things were getting worse. She was an anxious and worried person who spoke very little in consultations.

After spending a number of occasions sitting with her, she managed to describe that every day she saw the devil tormenting her. This frequent experience had shattered her ability to live independently. By listening to her experiences it became apparent that her medical diagnosis needed to be revised. This led to a change in her treatment plan and her medication. Although her experiences did not vanish she experienced a reduction in her suffering and her daily life became a little easier.

This situation challenged me. How should I approach the spiritual care of this lady? Spiritual care in various aspects of medicine is an important part of holistic care. From my own experience of prayer for people in church I believe she would have benefited from prayer and for the devil to be directly challenged (see Mark 16:17). Although I did not pray explicitly with her, I have prayed for her on a number of occasions since, in the confidence that God will hear my prayers (see Matthew 7:7-11). We are fortunate to have a health system that employs chaplains and she accepted my invitation to meet with them.

As a Christian psychiatrist I have had many Christians explore their understanding of mental illness with me. I have often found that they view mental illness differently from how they view physical illness. Somehow mental illness seems closer to what people would class as a "spiritual issue" compared with physical illness. The Bible teaches us that all suffering, whether it is physical or mental, is part of living in a fallen world.

Separating out the biological, psychological, spiritual and social aspects of humanity has led to many great advances in how we care for each other. However, these parts of us are not independent of each other. Where medical care has often fallen short is by over-emphasising one of these aspects to the detriment of others. A great challenge in modern medicine is to ensure that an individual's care does not neglect any of these aspects of being human.

When thinking about someone in church with a health problem I remember this instruction that James gives to the church:

> **'Is anyone among you sick? Let them call the elders of the church to pray over them and anoint them with oil in the name of the Lord.'** (James 5:14)

I learned a lot about this when I took the opportunity to visit a large missionary organisation in Mozambique. We spent our time there with the medical team who would run clinics for the local communities.There were many tales of both miraculous healing and successful medical treatments.

Those leading the clinics taught us about having discernment when treating those that are unwell. Often God moved in unexpected ways. Sometimes a simple physical ailment would reveal a larger spiritual difficulty, while sometimes an overt spiritual problem would reveal the need for physical care. I learned that when people are unwell we are called as their church to help in a holistic way. If you have an illness, mental or physical, do not neglect either the spiritual, medical or social care that others can offer. God is greater than we can ever imagine and wants to provide for us even more than a father wants to provide for his children (see Matthew 7:9-11).

A problem that many of my patients experience is that their perception of reality causes them extreme distress. Sometimes this may be more or less obvious. I recently treated someone who became dangerously dehydrated because they believed there was a rat inside their stomach and were refusing to eat or drink. Some untruths are subtler. Psychology describes these as "cognitive distortions". These happen commonly when someone is depressed and the thoughts that they have are overly negative. For example, they may be convinced that a future event is going to go badly despite everyone doing everything they can to plan for a good event.

In a similar way, I often have to think about my own worries in life and question which thoughts are more or less true. How can I test my thoughts and how can I know what is true? I praise Jesus that He reached into our broken world proclaiming, 'I am the way, the truth and the life' (see John 14:6).

Exploring the adventure of relationship with God through work

Occupation: Teacher

I have been teaching for seven years and, although I have heaps to learn, I have known God leading me at work especially through hard times and some big decisions.

Part way through my second year of reading law at university (which I hated) I found myself at the careers fair. I was brandishing a bag of glossy brochures but feeling pretty hopeless. I was about to leave when the person I was with bounded up to me saying that he had found what I was going to do with my life and that, 'it is going to be amazing.' It was one of those moments when I knew I had to listen, so I agreed to stay for ten more minutes.

I reached a stand promoting an organisation called Teach First. Within minutes I was sold! Teach First is an organisation that provides an expedited route into teaching at some of the most challenging inner-city schools in the country. The values of this organisation lined up with what I was passionate about – justice, education and cities. It was the perfect match.

If I am honest I had a bit of an idyllic image of being an adored, successful, inspiring teacher, humbly leading children to greatness.

In reality, though, my career certainly does not resemble that ideal. The experiences I have gained, however, have shown me so much more about God's priorities, including His care and sovereignty.

When you apply for Teach First you do not choose a school or an area. I simply had a choice between Manchester (home at the time) and London (a vast unknown). At interview I was put on the spot to make a decision. I prayed quickly, asking God what I should do. I heard Him clearly say, 'it is your choice, but London is the adventure.' Uncharacteristically I chose the adventure and I have been learning to choose adventure rather than comfort and safety ever since.

At points when London is at its most difficult (for example, packing to move for the hundredth time because the rental market in London is unpredictable, or saying goodbye to dear friends because London is so transient) God gently and lovingly reminds me that I chose the adventure, and that there is nowhere safer to be than adventuring with Him.

When I moved to London God provided a flat that allowed me an easy journey to work and also the proximity to be able to join and be involved with Revelation Church; things seemed great. Then I turned up for my first day of teaching and ended the day sobbing in the head's office, asking to resign. She convinced me to stay, but things did not really improve for a while.

Two years of high stress levels, lots of change, violent students, personal humiliation and complete exhaustion taught me more than I will ever teach those in my classroom. It was certainly not the idyllic view of teaching I had previously imagined.

God humbled me, softened me, toughened me up, opened my eyes and grew me dramatically in my time at that school. It was a painful process but a crucial one. I had to work through a lot of questions:

- Why had God placed me at the worst school possible, especially when I could easily have been placed somewhere else?
- If God was a good Father who wanted to protect me, why was I experiencing regular physical intimidation and assault?
- If God promised to give me all I needed, why was I running on empty?

What God showed me was that He was in the midst of it with me. He truly was Immanuel, *God with us*. The lunchtimes when I was crying and praying at my desk and things were being thrown at my windows, He was with me. The fun nights out with friends that I missed out on in order to make sure that I had my work done, He was with me. He never left me or abandoned me (see Deuteronomy 31:6, Joshua 1:5 and Isaiah 41:10-13).

One February evening, during my second year of teaching (my two compulsory Teach First years were nearing an end), I was rushing to a church meeting. It was dark and damp, but as I hustled down the street I looked up and saw a school building. I heard God say, 'go inside and ask if they have a job for you.' There are very few times I have heard God as clearly as I did that night and I would love to say I obeyed Him but I did not. I decided I was delusional and rushed on, forgetting all about it.

A couple of months later, work was still tough so while visiting family my mum staged an intervention. My job was consuming me, it was too much and I needed to get out so I agreed to do a few job searches to placate her. I found a school specialising in my subject that wanted a new head of department. It was double my salary, a Church of England school and closer to where I was living: I hurriedly wrote the application, dashing back to London to hand-deliver it.

I went in to drop off the letter but it was only when I looked up from my map, as I approached the school building, that I realised it was the same one God had spoken to me about a couple of months before. I ended up being given the job, and later finding out that they had interviewed and failed to appoint twice before I applied. In that experience I learned so much about God's grace and love for me. He is patient and kind, and I could move jobs knowing I was not running away from failure but being called into something new.

I had high hopes for this job and in many ways my five years there have been wonderful. God has taught me about putting down roots and committing to work but He has also taught me about the fragility of placing my identity in work, relying on it to define how important I am and how secure my life is.

Three years into this job the school decided to cut my department, something I had built, sacrificed for and poured myself into.

At that time I knew I had a choice: cut and run, or dig in and keep building. In God's strength I stayed and trusted that He was in control and that my work did not define me. *He did.* In two years He has more than restored what was lost.

I will soon be starting a new job as an Assistant Head Teacher locally. Exciting and terrifying as that prospect is, I know that this does not change how God sees or knows me, or what He is asking of me. I am asked to love justice, seek mercy and walk humbly with my God (see Micah 6:8). I am called to love my students, colleagues and community by being patient and kind, by not being arrogant or irritable, by rejoicing in the truth and by hoping and enduring all things (see 1 Corinthians 13).

My conviction around these things does not change from job to job or from workplace to workplace. They are simultaneously simple and profound, taking a lifetime to work out in practice. God has never left or forsaken me and has been with me at glorious moments and times of work-induced despair. Adventuring with God at work, as in all parts of life, remains exciting, challenging and the best way to approach living life in all of its fullness.

God's love in the charity sector

Occupation: Events and VIP Manager
for an international development charity

Working in the charity sector is not how I imagined it would be; it is better in many ways but also more challenging than I anticipated.

I have worked for two very different charities: a British medical charity and a development charity working in the Middle East. In both situations, I have found that people are often motivated to work in the charitable sector because of an emotive connection with the cause, a personal affiliation with the people being supported and a satisfaction from working for an ethical organisation. This means that people are generally very passionate about their job and often overworked. Many believe so strongly in the cause that they devote their whole life to it.

I fell into this narrative in my first few years of employment and God had to teach me early on in my career that my value is not derived from my work. He showed me that my identity does not come from what I produce and that it is not hidden in the cause I am working for.

It is, however, found in the fact that I am first and foremost His child and it is this truth that brings true rest. I might be busy and passionately working to further an ethical goal but I do not need to prove anything to others or myself and it is from this restful place that I am much more effective as a colleague, worker and friend in the workplace.

I have realised my need to depend completely on God for the challenges I face at work. As I mentioned, charities are full of passionate people and this can result in many strong opinions. Strong opinions combined with overworked professionals can lead to a pretty fiery environment. Zealous individuals often direct their outrage at injustices towards their colleagues.

I am learning to depend on God daily for the grace I need to do my job well and to respond appropriately in the face of these challenges. By studying the Bible and making time for prayer before I go to work each day I am able to manage this much more graciously.

The charity sector has exposed me to a lot of suffering around the world and it has had a big impact on me, especially as a Christian. My emotions have been pushed and pulled in many different directions as injustices stir up righteous anger within me.

I have witnessed children dying of long-term sickness, and wept as I have watched parents slowly lose their beloved child.

I have also seen children facing the consequences of a breakdown in politics in their region: homes are bombed at night while people sleep, family members are killed or dismembered from shrapnel, and when the sun rises those that have survived are left to face the devastation alone; traumatised teenagers wet their bed because they are terrified of being bombed again; and babies become malnourished due to the man-made political stalemate affecting food supplies to poverty-stricken families.

I recently visited a particularly troubled region in the Middle East and heard local Christians asking, 'Where is God in this?' One man said to me, 'I pray to God, but God cannot help here.' Their vision is so consumed by the affliction they face that they cannot conceive of God being bigger than their circumstances.

In these moments it is easy for me also to look at the situation, feel overwhelmed and wonder where God is. However, on these occasions I have cried out to Him; I have prayed and waited for wisdom and guidance to know how to respond and how to bring His comfort, and thankfully He has often given me specific prophetic words for colleagues. These have been able to bring timely comfort in tough situations.

There have also been times when He has reminded me, often through His word, that He is a God who cares deeply for the poor, the sick and the oppressed. I hold resolutely onto these promises in order to get perspective and keep hope (see Psalms 9:9, 14:6-7 and 16).

I find the Bible is full of reminders of God's deep love for the broken, His passion for justice and the truth that He has overcome all evil. Scripture tells us of His faithful love given freely for everyone. These verses are a powerful encouragement to me when I am surrounded by suffering.

In addition to prayer and Scripture, the Holy Spirit has often spoken clearly. I was recently overwhelmed by a colleague facing relentless suffering in the context of the work we do. She is an atheist so has no faith or God to hope in. She was shouting loudly, swearing at the injustice she faced and I could not find any words to respond. So I listened but felt pretty helpless.

Then she looked at me and declared, 'You are holy!' Her face softened and she smiled. She said she was encouraged to see holiness in a person when there was so much corruption surrounding her. I was shocked as I had not said a word about my faith and she did not know I was a Christian. I was soberly reminded that the Holy Spirit is working through us even though we may be completely unaware. My faith and hope were built up knowing He could soften and reveal Himself to any heart.

I am learning to be increasingly dependent on the Holy Spirit to help me in every moment. I have made many mistakes in the past by responding in my own strength, but He enables me to be a blessing for those facing much suffering.

The Bible reminds me that there is One who suffered (see Isaiah 53) more than any human will ever have to so that we might know true freedom and eternal life (see 2 Corinthians 5:21 and John 3:16). Jesus is the only Rock on which I can stand when all around me seems corrupt and unjust.

We see so much suffering in our broken world but there is a future hope that is greater than all these things: Jesus. When He returns He promises there will be no more hunger or thirst, and He will be our Shepherd. He will heal us, restore us, and will wipe every tear from our eyes (see Revelation 7:16-17).

FAITH AT WORK

I am privileged to work in a sector and region of the world where I can know God is present in suffering. I am passionate about the causes I work for but I am more passionate about bringing the ultimate hope to the people I work with.

God of my setbacks

Occupation: Registered Nurse

Auckland, New Zealand, is where I call home. After graduating from nursing I started practising at Auckland City Hospital and during this time I also completed my postgraduate studies in advanced nursing.

I am a planner and so when I started my first nursing job, I developed a five-year career plan. This included moving to London after two years of working full-time. However, my set plans and God's far better, life-shaping plans were not in sync. Something of Proverbs 19:21 became a reality for me where it says, 'many are the plans in a person's heart, but it is the Lord's purpose that prevails.'

As per my five-year career plan, I started my application for a UK nursing registration but after two years I was still a long way from completing it. I did not anticipate such a delay, but looking back now I can confidently say that it was all within God's timing. So after four years of working full-time I was ready for my big adventure and flew to London.

As an experienced nurse (having already done four years as a nurse in New Zealand), this involved taking, what felt like, a backwards step in my career because I was now working under those with less experience than myself. This was both humbling and challenging. I essentially returned to being a nursing student and also worked as a healthcare assistant until my registration was issued.

I requested assistance from universities to help me find my student placement but was left unaided, being advised that they could not enrol me prior to finding a placement. Thankfully though, within a couple of weeks God provided me with a job at one of London's biggest teaching hospitals where I was able to complete my clinical hours (the required on-the-job training/experience) and gain my UK nursing registration.

It was tough being a student nurse and healthcare assistant while waiting for my registration. Using the pain assessment scale of 0-10 (a measure we often use with patients in hospital: zero being no pain and ten being the most unbearable pain one could ever imagine), I would rate the ten months of my life as a nursing student and healthcare assistant as seven out of ten. My life at work was not always dreadful, but overall it was grim and depressing.

Firstly, the delayed process of registration led me to being apathetic and worn out. I struggled to find complete rest in God. Secondly, I felt that my value and identity were being undermined. It was frustrating that my nursing competency had to be validated, despite four years of experience before coming to the UK.

It is embarrassing to say but it would have been hard to believe that I was a Christian some days at work due to my attitude. I needed freedom and liberation from bitterness towards work. I needed to be reminded afresh of God's mighty plans for me.

The importance of identity in God

On reflection, I accepted the hierarchical culture in the medical field and considered being a healthcare assistant lower than the nursing status I thought I deserved. Biblical reflection led me to realise that I had my mind on things that the flesh desires rather than things that the Spirit desires (see Romans 8:5).

I needed to remember that my identity is in Christ and not in my position or skill as a nurse. This meant that:

- I was not defined by my uniform; worldly status does not matter to God. My Father sees me primarily as His daughter, and loves to join with me in serving others through nursing.

- I was not defined by my responsibility; God gives me many opportunities to make a difference and influence the patients, patients' family and colleagues regardless of my position.
- I was not defined by how quickly I progressed; God walks with me through a journey – time is not an issue for him.

Being a living sacrifice of worship through work

I also learned that, in whatever I do and regardless of my seniority, I should do my best and for God, presenting myself as a living sacrifice to Him (see Romans 12:1 and Colossians 3:23).

Living a life of sacrifice has meant:

- Acting in a way that is honouring to God. For example, it is easy to complain with colleagues but I believe that refraining from that culture and setting a new culture of positivity and encouragement is what God is asking of me.
- Reflecting the character of Christ at work and asking expectantly to grow compassion, joy and patience in my heart, particularly for the patients that I am helping.
- Giving thanks to God, even for little things and praising Him for them. Recently, I have even given thanks for the toilet flushing properly at work – we have had many plumbing issues in our ward!

God wants to be involved in our work

Eventually I learned to respond to the frustrations I faced with prayer. I learned that things do not always pan out as you might want them to and, though circumstances change, God was and is and will be the same faithful, loving, gracious and almighty Father. He cares and He wants to be involved in our circumstances, including our work.

Our prayers may be awkward, our attempts may be feeble, but the power of prayer is in the One who hears it and not in the one who says it. As a result, our prayers do make a difference. In my case, it was prayer that reconfigured my thinking and helped me to see how much God valued what I was doing, even if at times I struggled with what seemed like such a backwards step.

Conclusion

I have been challenged to seek no other identity than that which God has given me through Christ Jesus and I have been challenged to be a living sacrifice offered up to please God. God has graciously lifted the shame and embarrassment I felt looking back at my attitude towards work and I am now free to work with my eyes focused on God. I am now able to turn this all back to God in praise for what He has done in and through me.

> 'Because your love is better than life, my lips will glorify you. I will praise you as long as I live, and in your name I will lift up my hands.'
> (Psalm 63:3-4)

Work and ambition

_____

Renewed ambition

Occupation: Deputy Team Manager
for a family support service

Being ambitious is often seen as positive. I was always encouraged to strive for the best by my parents and I loved the positive attention I received from others for my achievements. My parents and my siblings are all very talented and my two eldest sisters set the mark high for me as the third daughter.

We are all very different and there is a notable age gap between us so it was not the competition that drove us – high achievement was the norm and was expected by our mum and dad. It was our parents' approval that drove us. We began competing against ourselves, always striving to be better. I would not dare come home with a bad mark or report.

Ever since my first year as a psychology undergraduate, I wanted to become a clinical psychologist. My studies, my free time and my jobs after university were geared towards this – if I could get the right experience in the first few years after graduating, I could get onto the training course. My career plan was all thought out and all I had to do was work hard.

As time went on, I gained some invaluable experience, but each year I applied to get onto the clinical training course my application was rejected. On a couple of occasions, I had come so close to getting an assistant psychologist job (considered the best experience for candidates applying for the clinical course) but lost out at the final interview stage.

I would drop everything when a new assistant psychologist post was advertised in order to complete the application, such was the importance of realising my dream of becoming a clinical psychologist. I told myself, 'unless I have a qualification, I do not have anything specific to define myself.' I wanted to hear God say, 'clinical psychology is your purpose and you will accomplish it.'

Every now and then I recognised there was an issue with my desire for achievement but I could not unpick it until the Holy Spirit prompted me to choose it as the main focus of a church-wide pastoral course I attended last year. I knew where my ambition came from but I could not get rid of its grip. Getting on clinical psychology training had become an idol.

The thing about ambition as an idol is that it never satisfies you. Once you have achieved something, the achievement no longer seems important or worthy and you aim for the next big thing. I think that this unhealthy ambition came from a desire for recognition from others, which was ironic given that I was striving for success in a field that exists primarily to help others, not myself. I explored this in detail at our church's pastoral course and felt God speaking to me about renewing my ambition by placing my trust in Him because only He can satisfy.

> 'And the Lord will guide you continually and satisfy your desire in scorched places and make your bones strong; and you shall be like a watered garden, like a spring of water, whose waters do not fail.'
> (Isaiah 58:11)

At the same time as this pastoral course, our church ran a breakfast series looking at our faith in the workplace and I benefited from every one of the talks. During one session I picked up a paper entitled *Calling – A Biblical Perspective*, which looked at our purpose in life and was particularly helpful as it brought my focus back onto Jesus. A couple of quotes in particular really spoke to me:

> 'First and foremost we are called to Someone (God), not something (such as motherhood, politics or teaching) or somewhere (such as the inner-city or Mongolia).'
> (Os Guinness, The Call)

> 'God might lead you to a job you know nothing about, have no present knack for, and don't think you would like. Would you be willing to take that job? Conversely, you might discover late in life that you missed God's professional calling for you. Take heart, ... the calling to belong to Christ is God's only indispensible calling.'
> (Calling: A Biblical Perspective, Theology of Work Project)

Wow, this really spoke to me! Something just clicked. I was so blinded by the desire to become a clinical psychologist that I was not able to appreciate God's provision at work in the area of family support. Now looking at my job I can see not only how God placed me in a job I did not know even existed but also how I can fulfil my God-given potential and worship the "Someone" regardless of the fact that being a family support worker is not what I originally set out to do (see Colossians 3:23). In addition, all my previous roles have perfectly prepared me for this task.

I also started to learn to hold my career lightly, remembering that my identity is in Jesus Christ and not in my job title. This brings an amazing freedom and sense of peace, as we are not qualified as righteous ourselves, but rather we receive the righteousness of Jesus through what He did on the cross.

As I continued to grow in this new knowledge, God blessed me with a promotion I did not even dream of. I have now been Deputy Team Manager for eight months and I have excelled in the role, receiving a lot of praise. Yet for the first time in my life I recognised that these things are a gift from God.

In helping me to overcome unhealthy ambition, God has led me into greater fellowship and accountability through church community, small groups, courses, prayer partners, my marriage and family. He does not leave us to fend for ourselves, but empowers us with the Holy Spirit and gives us friends and family to help us persevere.

> 'As iron sharpens iron, so one person sharpens another.'
> (Proverbs 27:17)

I am still on a journey but God has been healing and restoring me. My renewed ambition is to serve God well in my workplace, wherever He takes me.

Beating idleness and the fear of failure

Occupation: Fashion Entrepreneur and part-time Youth Progression Manager

I remember moving back from Nigeria to London at sixteen and enrolling in the local college. I found it much easier than the rigorous and almost militant education system in Nigeria. For the first time ever, I barely had to study to ace tests and exams. Without any parental guidance to push me to apply myself and try harder I became complacent knowing that I could get away with the bare minimum and still achieve the straight As my mum in Nigeria wanted.

This complacency became second nature and bore a fruit of idleness, which followed me throughout university. Although I was forced to try harder to maintain my top grades and achieve a first in Mathematical Economics and Statistics, the mentality of avoiding hard work and doing the bare minimum became further ingrained in me.

This in turn bred a deep fear of failure because I knew that continuing to avoid hard work would some day lead to disastrous results. This fear was also further fuelled by the fact that I had spent years not applying myself and therefore did not have any real understanding of what I was capable of.

When I began my graduate job in the city I was confronted with the ugliness of my idleness and complacency. Working to deadlines and being accountable to my manager and my team meant that I could no longer avoid hard work and getting things done, but I soon realised that the fear of being seen as slow and unreliable at work was my motivation for doing my job, rather than pleasing God and delighting in the job He had given me. This meant that any effort that I put into my work was only skin deep, and only lasted as long as was necessary to keep my team and managers happy.

Three years and two job changes later, complacency and the fear of failure were still things that I struggled with when God gave me the vision for starting a fashion business. Starting a business requires a lot of hard work, self-discipline and the courage to take risks – all the things I had spent my life struggling with. Therefore, it was no surprise that I felt fearful stepping out into the vision that I believed God had given me. I could not stop thinking:

- 'Can I actually do this?'
- 'What if I fail?'
- 'Why would God bless me with a successful business when my habitual complacency and fear of failure make me so undeserving?'

Almost a year into embarking on this journey of setting up my own business I still sometimes have these thoughts but in every dark moment of doubt God has shone through, showing His love for me through confirming His will in multiple ways.

I am challenged by the Holy Spirit to trust that God's plans for me are perfect and good (see Jeremiah 29:11), that He will supply everything I need and that He is more than able to break the chains of sin in my life (see 2 Peter 1:3). God has also shown His fatherly love for me by 'chastising' me (see Hebrews 12:6) when I let my complacency and fear of failure paralyse me to the point of inaction.

I remember one particularly poignant occasion when I spent my entire day procrastinating. I immersed myself in the world of Netflix. I fought tooth and nail to ignore the nudging of the Holy Spirit who was calling me to activities that would be far more productive. My procrastination was an attempt to escape from the mountain of business tasks that had piled up but my escape did not give me peace.

At the end of the evening my husband returned from work and I was completely overcome with guilt and fear that my idleness had won and, as a result, my God-given vision would come to nothing. My husband asked me how my day had gone and I immediately burst into tears. The floodgates opened and I let out all the fear that I had been holding inside for months: fear of failure, inadequacy and the fear that my habitual sin of idleness had finally won. My husband and I prayed through my tears and he encouraged me to spend time with God.

After praying together I decided to pray on my own and study God's word. In that time God spoke to me very clearly: idleness and fear are not of God (see 2 Thessalonians 3:10 and 2 Timothy 1:7) and I am to hate laziness as much as God hates it and flee from it whenever it rears its ugly head.

When I have tried to break the cycle of idleness and the fear of failure through my own strength it has never worked because my motivation was not to please God but to please man (see Galatians 3:10).

God made it clear to me that it is by the grace of God that I will beat sin. I will be tempted on a daily basis but I will persevere through prayer and leaning on God's strength and not my own. I will trust in the Lord always because He will never forsake me (see Proverbs 3:5-6).

God also gave me a verse to meditate on daily:

> **'The soul of a sluggard craves and gets nothing, while the soul of the diligent is richly supplied.'** (Proverbs 13:4)

I had craved success and fulfillment but had nothing but a growing void, feelings of inadequacy and a lack of trust in the Lord. Now I have broken free by the grace of God from the chains that bound me so tightly and I rest in His promise to make me rich with purpose and unshakeable faith in the Lord.

Living in the moment, dreaming about the future

Occupation: Chartered Surveyor and Property Manager

There is a fine balance between living in the moment and aspiring for better in the future.

It is important to live in the present; to enjoy what you have now. This is what the Bible means by contentment. Contentment is being joyful in your current season, be it with a little or with plenty (see Philippians 4:11-13). However, the Bible also encourages us to prophesy, dream and have visions of the future (see Acts 2:17). God gives us dreams so that He can build faith in us but also because He wants us to live in the hope of knowing that He can do big things in us (see Ephesians 3:20-21).

I carry so many dreams for the future. From when I was very little I was always strongly encouraged to have goals and to do my best to achieve them. I remember my auntie giving me a book about planning for the future and having dreamboat goals. Dreamboat goals are those that may seem impossible but could be achieved.

Although this planning and goal-orientated family environment has very much helped me to achieve many things, I started to develop a sense of self-reliance that was not healthy. Despite great academic results from school, at university I started to attach a lot of my identity to what I achieved (or did not achieve for that matter). When life did not go to plan I found this devastating at times.

One such example was my plans to have a baby at twenty-eight. I soon found out that I had fertility problems and my plans were falling apart around me. At this time God spoke to me about dreaming of the future but trusting Him to give me the plans of my heart and, with patience and contentment, to trust in His timing (see Psalm 37:4-5). I started learning to delight myself in God's present grace while still carrying many hopes and dreams for the future.

God gives us desires, visions and dreams. He wants us to look to the future with hope. At the same time He wants us to surrender our hearts and visions to Him so that He can use us according to His purpose and will.

Over the last few years I have often thought about biblical principles on living in the present alongside planning, dreaming and waiting on God to fulfil promises. The four principles that I really value are below:

Pray
Dream
Plan
Commit

Pray

A good foundation before starting anything is to pray. Prayer is two-way. It involves pouring out your heart and your desires to God as well as listening to what He has to say to you. Praying the Father's heart into our work and daily lives reminds us that we are living, not for our careers, but to become more like Jesus as He transforms us from one degree of glory to another (see 2 Corinthians 3:18).

Praying helps us to live in the present. Prayer should contain thanksgiving to Jesus, thanking Him for daily grace, strength and provision. This regular thanksgiving helps us to remember the blessings that we currently have. It is good to regularly give thanks for God's provision and blessing no matter how little.

The most recent example from my life has been learning to enjoy the process of renovating my flat rather than living for the future state of completion. Once I came to this realisation, I felt prompted to give thanks to God for the blessing of these projects and asked him to help me enjoy the process. Soon, instead of despair at a long to-do list, God started to fill me with joy in the small details.

Dream

Dreaming is important because it enables us to use our faith. It encourages us to think about what the future could look like in our context. Dreaming stretches us beyond our current reality and into another realm of the impossible becoming possible.

However, it can be a very lonely place, dreaming of a miracle and submitting your dreams to God. God has gently and tenderly shown me that His timing is perfect and in His time He will fulfil the desires of our hearts according to His will.

I work in the property industry and I am passionate about transforming the way landlords manage their buildings and interact with their clients. There is a real desire and drive in me to continually improve standards in the industry. It is something that I dream about.

How am I going to see this achieved? To be honest, I am not always sure but this I know: to achieve it I must seek first the kingdom of God (see Matthew 6:33-34). In addition, the experience of waiting for a child has really laid a foundation of trusting God for seemingly impossible things and learning to wait in all aspects of my life, including work.

Plan

The principle of planning is very practical. It is a process of looking at your current position, understanding where you want to get to and mapping out a way to get there. For this process to be effective there should be goals that you are trying to reach.

Planning is clearly shown in the Bible to be a good thing (see Isaiah 30:1 and Proverbs 15:22, 16:9 and 21:5). God's planning principles (drawn from these verses) include being inspired by the Holy Spirit, seeking advice and taking time. Planning is the characteristic of someone who is not hasty or impatient. Planning should be undertaken by people who are prepared to ask for help; those who pray and ask God for direction and who do so patiently.

I have found it a very healthy practice to write annual or five-year plans. I do this by thinking about dreams that I want to see become a reality. I then identify the practical steps I need to take in order to achieve them.

Commit

After planning it is essential that we give our plans to God (see Proverbs 16:3) and say, 'Lord if this is your will please bless my plans.' Often we can make the most detailed plans of how the future will look and forget the Master of the universe is totally in control of our destiny.

I remember when I wanted to become a chartered surveyor, I had just found out I was pregnant and I felt God stir me to faith that He would carry me through the process of successfully becoming chartered, having a baby and working full-time. I felt such a profound grace on that period. I prayed and committed my way to Him. I kept committing my work to God knowing I needed Him to make me strong by His Spirit. I praise God for the strength He gave me to pursue these things.

Conclusion

God wants us to bask in His daily grace, even in the tough seasons. Appreciate the season you are in while dreaming of a better future. May God grant you your heart's desires and fulfil all your plans.

Work and worship

Taking great satisfaction in the work of your hands and using it as a way to display your faith at work

Occupation: Barber

'Whatever you do, work at it with all your heart, as working for the Lord, not for human masters.' (Colossians 3:23)

I never set out to be a barber. You might say it was accidental, but looking back I can see God had a plan.

I spent my childhood getting a haircut from my mother and older brothers until I reached an age when I thought I wanted more than just a grade zero all around or a one level with no shape-up. My family did not have the money to pay for proper haircuts, so when I was fourteen years old I picked up a pair of clippers myself for the first time and slowly improved at working with hair.

Two months after my eighteenth birthday, I was walking through my friend's neighbourhood and jokingly said to the manager of the local barbershop that I could cut better than one of his employees. I was genuinely joking but he took me literally and told me to come in and prove myself. I did not take him up on it, but in the following weeks, every time he saw me he would ask me when I was coming to work in the shop.

I really wanted to, but I was too scared to take up the opportunity in case I messed up a client's haircut.

One day the manager put me on the spot while the owner was there, telling him that I had declined his invite to work in the shop, so the owner said firmly that I should be there next Sunday. I thought to myself that since they were forcing me to come, I could not be blamed for messing up anyone's hair. So I went in that Sunday.

I always had a passion for helping people and serving the community, so barbering is not what I thought God had in mind for my career when I recommitted my life to Him at the age of twenty. Social work, or something along those lines, is how I saw myself living out my faith at work. So I began a course in social work, and developed my passion for barbering on the side, cutting in the barbershop part-time.

As a barber, you get to know a lot of people. You not only get to know your customers but you get to know everyone else within your interconnected sphere. I began cutting hair for friends, then it progressed to friends of friends, neighbours, colleagues, and generations of the same families: sons, fathers and grandfathers. I was not conscious at first of what God was doing, but slowly I began to realise that through barbering God had strategically placed me in a position of influence right at the heart of the Afro-Caribbean community in North London.

My faith at work does not involve preaching but rather simply trying to reflect the image of God in everything I do: my speech, honest business practice, a good work ethic, sharp haircuts, and the overall part I play in my community. In all these areas I have chosen to honour God and as a result I believe He has honoured me (see 1 Samuel 2:30). I have seen Him bring fruit and growth both financially and in terms of the influence I have in the community.

A barber is a bit like a therapist or a GP, only in a communal setting and for cosmetic purposes. While clients are in the chair they reveal all sorts of things: their problems, their opinions, the latest dramas and debates. Whether one-on-one with a client, or more publicly when the whole shop is discussing an issue, I am able to speak into people's lives and bring a godly perspective to things.

More than my speech, my actions have probably been the most important way that I have reflected Jesus in the community.

One of the best examples of this would be the way in which I have taken over responsibility for managing the shop, when nobody else was prepared to. After working there for a few years, I discovered the barbershop was in some debt and nobody seemed to want to take responsibility for the administration of the business. Although I was the youngest person working there, I took the responsibility of paying off the debts with my own money and I set up systems to get the administrative side running properly. If I had not stepped up, who knows what would have happened.

With no official structures in place, I inadvertently became the co-manager of the shop. I am now in a position of even more influence to impact both the wider community and the environment of the shop. I have been able to introduce things like no-swearing policies and I have had a say in what we allow to be shown on the TV. Overall, though, I have been able to create an environment that is godlier.

Another, more personal way that I have shown integrity in the shop has been by declaring my earnings honestly. The cash-in-hand nature of the business means that there is a big temptation to keep what you earn off the radar and pay no tax. I made a decision from the beginning to declare my earnings honestly and like Jesus said, 'Give to Caesar what is Caesar's' (see Mark 12:17).

People watching were not always very supportive of this and it was certainly going against the grain. However, in the long run, God has really honoured my honesty and it has actually left me in a better position because, with a credit rating, I have been able to get loans and mortgages that I would not otherwise have been able to if I had not declared my full earnings.

In a community where many people do not have parents or family with much experience of managing finance, I am now in a position where people come to me for advice on handling their money, getting mortgages and running their own businesses.

My professionalism as a barber has also had an impact on those around me. By simply being punctual and reliable, taking my job seriously, serving customers with respect, and consistently honing my craft, I have attracted more and more customers and my work has been brought to the attention of various celebrities who now also form part of my regular client list.

Another way in which I have chosen to honour God and reflect Him in my work has been through treating all my customers the same. There is a guy who used to come into our barbershop who was an alcoholic, had mental issues, never showered, did not wash his clothes, and even though he had a home, just sat on the pavement all day. He would come in smelling, with dirty skin, filthy clothes and filthy hair. Nobody wanted to cut his hair. I knew that it was my responsibility to treat him the same as everybody else – to take him on and cut his hair; not just a standard haircut, but a good haircut, and show him love. From then on he became my client and he would keep coming back to get a haircut from me.

It is only a haircut I am giving people, but God has taken this small seed and grown a big oak that branches out into areas I would never have imagined.

This is my faith at work.

Work and following
God's leading

Prayer, the prophetic and God's favour

Occupation: Real Estate Finance Investment Manager

'Give her the fruit of her hands and let her works praise her in the gates.' (Proverbs 31:31)

This is the story of an unexpected journey with God.

I always wanted to be a doctor (ever since I was five years old) and I spent the next fifteen years ensuring I did every type of relevant work experience possible; I truly felt called to be a doctor. Two universities offered me a place on their course and my whole life was mapped out.

I come from a particularly gifted family academically: three generations of Oxbridge graduates, top five in the country for some exams, skipping years at school, top first honours, top jobs at Goldman Sachs (the list goes on) – it is all pretty sickening really. You can imagine the family reunions!

However, God has not gifted me that way and I failed to get the required grades for medicine. It was at this stage that I decided to go through clearing to study molecular biology, with the hope of switching after the first year onto medicine or at the least doing a second degree in medicine. However, in the summer between my first and second year my mum was diagnosed with terminal cancer and I decided I could not face a second degree.

In my final year I came upon a scheme with a financial organisation that focused on commercial property finance. This seemed like a good idea and I successfully gained a place.

When I first started working I did not know anything about the sector. I was pretty insecure and competitive – this does not make for a very pleasant combination. I remember asking God to help me be more gracious and so God provided me with challenging situations so I could learn. It took several years of graft to grow this fruit. One very important thing I learned in this time was to delight in other people's successes and once I did I realised the freedom that this gave me.

Four years into my job and I began to feel quite unsettled. However, I knew God had given me this job and I wanted above all to honour him. At this time a prophetic word was given at the front of my local church and I knew it was for me. After the service I sought out the person that gave it, explained my situation and asked God to give me clarity over my job. Being honest with God I asked Him to make it really clear so that I did not make the wrong decision.

The next day at work my boss called me into a meeting, told me that the company really valued me and that I would be given an immediate pay rise and put on a special bonus scheme that would aim to keep significant people for a three year period. God definitely gave me the clarity I requested!

With one more year before the bonus was paid out, I was getting bored and looking for another challenge. I was still keen not to end up working long-term in banking. Over that period I was meeting with some women in my church small group to pray and mentioned that I was feeling quite restless in my job. One of them immediately said that God had told her I was going to move jobs and in addition she had had a dream where I was surrounded by money. I prayed and weighed this prophetic word and felt peaceful about moving jobs.

While considering my move, I prayed about some specific things – I asked God for great managers, for the job to come to me rather than the other way round and that God would make it really clear that this was the job He wanted me to take. I met with a few recruiters and one told me I would be crazy to move before the bonus was paid, but God had spoken and I felt completely at peace. 'Surely God had a better plan,' I resolved.

The job I ended up taking had all of the things that I prayed for and on top of this they paid me out of my bonus, something I had not even prayed for. God's lavish love and grace overwhelmed me.

Before starting the new job I took the weekend before to pray and fast. I was confident that God had put me there for a reason. The job was in an investment management team at a small advisory firm. I felt completely unqualified and out of my depth. Frankly, I felt that I did not even deserve the job. The knowledge that God had given me the job is what sustained me. In addition, He gave me some incredible support from people that I had met in the industry (many who told me to call them whenever I needed).

In my first week, it was announced that the client had won three major deals and that one of them was from the firm I had just left. As such, I was immediately able to provide insight. I saw this as another confirmation that God had given me the job.

What God showed me over the next year really changed my perspective on what God thinks of the workplace:

- He showed me huge favour, something I specifically prayed for but was given in truly miraculous ways. The client that we were working with took extra notice of me and would phone my bosses to ensure that I was working on their projects.
- In tricky situations, God softened hearts and changed outcomes. This happened both with colleagues and clients and in all cases it was pretty instant.
- Most miraculously though, God gave me words of knowledge for my colleagues. Moreover, I was able and confident to act on them and I believe they had an incredible impact on those that they were for.

All the situations above were rooted in prayer. During the difficult times I would go to the bathroom several times a day to pray and be filled with the Spirit.

I continued to meet weekly with my accountability partner to pray and talk about life but with a particular emphasis on work. I began reading the book of Daniel to deepen my understanding of what God thinks about the workplace and I attended a workplace breakfast series that our church put on. I did these things to be encouraged and to learn from those further on the journey.

You may be thinking that this all sounds rather idyllic. In truth I also encountered much spiritual attack in this season. I believe this was a result of taking ground for the kingdom. In those times it was vital that I had regular fellowship and encouragement. There were even a few times I thought about leaving but God was always bigger and greater than the attack and I had people around me that were able to see it clearly for what it was.

So what would I like you to remember from this story? God is faithful, willing and able to miraculously impact on work life. Your colleagues, clients and contacts will be impacted by the love of God. Be expectant about how God will use you and in everything you do be devoted to prayer, the word and fellowship.

> 'Do you see a man skilful in his work? He will stand before kings; he will not stand before obscure men.' (Proverbs 22:29)

Trust God and follow His prompting

Occupation: TV Editor

Since being a teenager I have loved being creative with video. Aged eighteen I moved to London from Southampton to study contemporary media practice at the University of Westminster.

I completed my first year and due to some long-term health issues I was unable to return to university until half way through my second year. On my return I spoke to my tutor about my future. I told him I wanted to be an editor. He said to me that there was not much point in coming back to university and that I should go and get a job as a runner at a post-production company.

I was shocked at his honesty. I thought it was important to have a degree to get anywhere in life. It turns out it is more important to trust God with everything. I made the call to drop out of university and the search for entry-level jobs began.

I spent several fruitless months applying for every job available. I eventually decided I needed another approach. I decided to print twenty copies of my CV, attach a handwritten letter and post them to all the editors at a particular post-production company. It worked! I started work in July 2010. I trusted God and He came through (and that was not the last time).

In 2010 this was the verse I held on to in hope and expectation:

> 'Trust in the Lord with all your heart, and lean not on your own understanding. In all your ways acknowledge him, and he will make your paths straight.' (Proverbs 3:5)

It has been situations like this that mean I can now hold on to this verse knowing it is true and God is faithful when you put your whole trust in Him.

During the early days in this job I was regularly praying with a friend. He shared how God spoke to him that I would find favour in my workplace like Joseph did in Egypt (see Genesis 30-50). I have never forgotten that moment and I carry that promise to this day.

During my first few weeks I made an effort to introduce myself to every editor and producer. I worked as hard as I could. I did training either side of my eight-hour running shifts just to get ahead. I had the attitude that on the basis I had dropped out of university early I needed to make the most of the opportunity God had given me. I tried to operate with this Scripture in mind:

> 'Whatever you do, work heartily, as for the Lord and not for men, knowing that from the Lord you will receive the inheritance as your reward.' (Colossians 3:23)

I was told there was no way that I would become an editor within five years; it was an impossibility and unheard of. However, all I had ringing in my ears was that I would find favour like Joseph.

Within the space of six months I was promoted twice to edit assistant. It was unheard of – yes – but it was the favour God promised. It spurred me on and I found myself praying harder, working harder and developing a passion to see God move powerfully to redeem the TV industry.

I have a tendency to think that my achievements are based on my abilities. My wife is incredible at gently reminding me that it was God that provided these opportunities and that He is the reason I found favour at this post-production company. He gives us skills and abilities and then helps us put them to good use for His glory (see Deuteronomy 8:18).

Two years later and an editor role opened up. I was definitely not the obvious choice. However, I had an outside chance and applied. I got the job! I believed God for His promise and He came through (and that was not the last time).

I was completely out of my depth, working on some of the biggest programmes out there but God was with me. If He had given me this opportunity He would give me the skills to do it. He did.

A combination of the type of work I was doing (I was frustrated) and a suggestion from a friend about going freelance challenged my thinking about what to do next.

I put it off for a while but eventually I called an agency. It was just an enquiry, but an enquiry and a conversation later this was starting to look like a real possibility.

I tried the idea on my wife, then my family and then a few close church friends. Everyone seemed so positive about the idea. I could not believe that for once I was the only one being cautious and everyone else was being crazy. I think it was God's way of having a bit of fun with me; the only time I can ever remember being cautious, the cautious people God put around me were all pushing me.

After a difficult conversation with the managing directors, I handed in my notice. They were disappointed and I was sad about that. For over five years I had loved working there. I had some incredibly fond memories and some great friends. I have a huge amount of gratitude for the company.

I found myself looking again at the Scripture in Proverbs 3:5. My wife and I trusted that God was in this and, willingly and as wisely as possible, followed His leading. I did not have months of work lined up but we knew God was leading and we had to follow.

God turned my first freelance job into an opportunity to test my motives for going freelance. The first show I got offered was a show called *Love Island*. I knew exactly what the show entailed and I did not feel comfortable working on it. The thing was that the money was fantastic and I had no other work booked. The money would have been enough for the next four months. My wife and I both knew it was not right.

We just did not have peace about it and knew that this was not the type of show I should be working on. I turned it down.

The next job was on a show called *Ex on the Beach*. It was the same deal all over again; great money but it did not feel right. We prayed, 'God we trust you with this situation, would you provide the work.'

Within the next week I had work booked up for the next four months and on shows that I really wanted to work on. I decided to do the right thing and He came through again (and that was not the last time). I hope you are beginning to spot the recurring theme!

The thing I have learned most through the early part of my career is that the best place we can be in is a place of complete trust in God for every area of our lives and in everything acknowledging Him (see Proverbs 3:5-6). If we ever start to think we can do it on our own we start to fall apart.

God is good all the time and wants us to trust and share every area of our lives with Him.

Faith to follow God's lead

Occupation: TV Producer

I began my career with a clear sense of calling. In the midst of hearing someone speak on righteous anger it was as if a compass had stopped spinning wildly and hit due north.

God was speaking to me about politics.

This sounds great, except for the fact that I had barely picked up a newspaper in my life! I applied for an internship working for an MP and, miraculously, got the job. I was all set to change the world. However, it turns out that life, and politics, is a lot more complicated than that.

Fast forward a few years and I had a career in political consultancy (or lobbying to use the less appealing title!) and was working my way up the ladder.

The problem was, I was really unhappy (for a number of reasons that I will not go into here) and increasingly torn between knowing that God had led me to where I was and also feeling a very real heaviness about staying in the job that I was in. I also had an increasing desire to work in broadcast rather than consultancy.

At the same time, my husband was pursuing a career in a notoriously tough industry, where breakthrough can take a long time. We were relying on my salary, a decision made before God (to be clear: my husband's heart to provide was very much in the right place).

The upshot of all this was that I felt trapped.

I did not understand how to reconcile God's original leading for me to work in politics with being in a place that felt so barren and that was having such a negative impact on me emotionally. Being motivated and diligent at work was a real struggle and, while I was being promoted and having good appraisals, I was not giving my all.

In the midst of this struggle, God spoke to me about freshly understanding what it meant for Him to be the Bread of Life. I was reminded of Exodus 16 where God rains blessing on the Israelites in the form of fresh bread *each day* but they are only to gather for the day itself. I had a sense that fresh bread (in the form of leaving my job) was coming and it was a lesson to me that if change did come I was to continue relying on God daily, rather than trusting in the new stability/season of blessing.

This was particularly pertinent for me in the case of finances. When you are paid monthly (even if things are looking financially tight and even if you are not enjoying how you earn it) it can be very easy to "sort of" know that provision comes from God but not to be actively aware of this. People often talk about the heart risks of being very wealthy but money can have just as much of a grip on you through fear of not having enough.

For a long time I had felt that I had to stay in my job because I needed to provide financially but God had been gently working on my heart to show me that He is our Provider and to teach me what that actually means.

Over the years, my husband and I had talked and prayed regularly about the situation but it had never felt right for me to leave.

I think it is worth noting here that, in general, I do not think that there is a prescribed right or wrong for whether you should stay in a job that you do not like. Sometimes God might be calling us to stay, persevere and push through and sometimes it might be right for us to get out. However, I do believe that we are called to honour those we work for and that God gives us freedom to make decisions in our lives, as long as we are being obedient to His call.

For me, things reached a head after I had been in my job for four and a half years. I was leaving work on a Friday not excited that it was the weekend but rather dreading having to go back on Monday morning.

It is hard to describe exactly what shifted but it began to feel like the situation was not sustainable. We sought counsel from close friends and those with more experience than us (including our parents) and felt like God was moving us towards taking a step of faith and me handing in my notice. I had no experience in broadcast (the industry I wanted to go into) and no job lined up.

There were a few key things that really helped with our decision:

1. **Prayer.** A lot of prayer. We prayed and people we loved and respected prayed for us.

2. **Let the peace of Christ rule in your hearts.** Colossians 3:15 calls us to let the peace of Christ rule in our hearts. A very wise leader at our local church said to us that often the framework for biblical decision-making is to be proactive. Rather than waiting for God to tell me, 'now is the time to leave,' we should say, 'God, we think that perhaps it is right for me to hand in my notice. We submit this decision to you, we invite you to change and shape our thinking, to lead us and to stop us in our tracks if this is wrong,' and through this to let His peace rule in our hearts as we make the decision.

3. **There are no detailed maps.** A friend had a picture for us, which in essence spoke of God not being in the business of handing out detailed maps for our lives. Rather, He wants to reveal the big promises He has made and for us to make decisions with our eyes fixed on Him and the big picture. If we are waiting for a step-by-step guide we are unlikely to get it but if, like Samson, we look to use our gifts humbly for His glory then God will guide us in that.

4. **Fix your eyes on Jesus.** In Judges 13 an angel appears to Manoah's wife and speaks to her about what is to come from God. However, she and Manoah wanted to hear it again and ask for more. God in His kindness lets the angel repeat what was said but does not give any new information. The angel then points them back to make a

sacrifice to God. It was another reminder that if we fix our eyes on Jesus, we do not need to get hung up on the details. We came to the point where, simply put, we had peace about me leaving my job, even though it was scary.

So, despite not having a job to go to, no guarantee of money coming in and wanting to get into a completely different career, I handed in my notice.

It was terrifying but one of the best decisions I have ever made. Since then, God has faithfully opened door after door into a new industry and I am now working full-time as a TV producer, doing what I really want to do.

I may not have followed a conventional route but not only was God teaching me some powerful lessons – about His goodness, provision, timing and care – but also, I was gaining experiences and skills that enabled me to make a sideways step into an industry that is very difficult to break into. I was expecting to be starting from scratch making the tea!

Most of all, I have learned more about trusting God.

He is a faithful Father.

Believe and obey

Occupation: Youth Hub Co-ordinator

'Trust in the LORD with all your heart and lean not on your own understanding.' (Proverbs 3:5)

Your career and your life is a journey. It may not end up working out how you imagined it to but if you choose to listen to God and submit your plans and purposes to Him, He will take you on an adventure to places that you may never have thought you would go and give you experiences that you probably did not think possible. This is because He knows the absolute best for His children.

This is my testimony. Throughout my career He has been so faithful in helping me in every step and at every junction or crossroad, however difficult.

My journey started with a design degree. I disqualified myself from doing something academic (even though social work and young people were my real passions) and I spent three enjoyable years studying the intricacies of interior design.

Recently graduated and newly married, I needed to provide an income that paid the bills. The pressure was on to find a job. I applied for numerous roles and submitted many CVs and applications. I even managed to get some work experience in an interior design firm. However, it just seemed that every door that I pushed in the creative industry just did not want to open.

While I was decorating my Nan's house (a little job on the side to bring in some money) God spoke to me so clearly about what He wanted me to do; it was one of those light bulb moments. I realised that I was actually more passionate about the local youth project that I was involved with and helping the vulnerable young people there. Rather than following what seemed like the most logical career path, I decided to look for jobs working with homeless young people.

I had all the wrong credentials but God soon provided me with a job working in a London borough for one of the largest homeless outreach hostels. I worked there for a year as a support worker. In addition, God showed me that my degree was not a waste of time. I was able to put my skills to good use by running some art workshops. I even helped the young people create a t-shirt design business.

During this time my love for young people grew immensely but God also started to give me a much wider vision for what could be achieved in the social sector, giving me lots of dreams and ideas.

God stepped it up and all the thoughts and plans He had given me were confirmed through an amazing prophetic word that someone gave me. God was enlarging my vision and my heart even further for the purposes I believed He had for me.

After praying and reflecting on this word I became restless in my current job and asked God what the next step was in fulfilling what he had promised. God gave me a two-word phrase, which unknown to me at the time was the name of the organisation that my friend had just got a new job working for. This was no coincidence. God was at work directing and shaping my next steps. I wasted no time in getting online and I found a job being advertised for a support worker position working with vulnerable young people in the same London borough that I was already working in. I applied, got an interview and then the job. God really provided.

During my first year in this role, I was given two promotions and before long I found myself as part of the management team. I was twenty-three and I was already managing a service for fifty young people (including young mothers and their children) and overseeing the ten staff members involved. God spoke to me powerfully through the following verse of Scripture:

'Do not let people look down on you because you are young, but set an example.' (1 Timothy 4:12)

God gave me the grace to do things I never thought I would ever be able to. I learned that it does not matter how old you are or how unable you might feel because He gives you the skills and abilities to do things you could never think or imagine (see Deuteronomy 8:18).

I hope you are beginning to see the repeating pattern of God at work in my life: He speaks, I listen and then respond and walk by faith into His plans and promises, praising Him for His faithfulness as He fulfills what He has spoken in my life.

During this time, my husband and I decided to spend a week away discussing God's plans for our future. The last night of our holiday God woke me up very vividly and said, 'this is not my plan, I want you to start trying for a baby.'

I questioned God. This was not my desire for now. How were the dreams that He had placed in my heart so clearly now going to be fulfilled? Knowing that this was what God wanted, I had to lay down my aspirations, believing that God's timing is perfect in fulfilling His purposes. Even if we have to sacrifice things, when we trust in God, He leads us to pastures. Faith is sometimes about the waiting for what we do not know or yet have.

Faith in God requires courage to step up and courage to trust Him. God has shown me that when we ask, listen and obey, He provides. Our careers are journeys with many twists, turns, ups and downs but God is faithful to fulfil His promises. Always!

I am excited to see the fulfillment of the promises from God that are yet to be realised, spurred on by the many promises and prophetic words I have already seen fulfilled in my life and career so far.

Work and church/mission

Work as a means to developing a discipline for voluntary use where it is most needed

Occupation: Junior Doctor

I purposely did not study medicine when I went to university because I always hated biology.

During my first degree I felt challenged to rethink my priorities: what would it look like to give my life to God in full-time service? If the only decision that really matters in this life is how we respond to Jesus, surely time spent pursuing anything other than making Jesus known is wasted?

I love reading biographies of past missionaries who gave everything to preach the good news of Jesus where He was not known. The following Scripture was of particular inspiration to me:

> 'How, then, can they call on the one they have not believed in? And how can they believe in the one of whom they have not heard? And how can they hear without someone preaching to them?'
> (Romans 10:14)

Much of East Asia is "unreached": millions live in fear of spirits whom Jesus defeated thousands of years ago, yet they have never had the opportunity to hear of Him. On graduating, through a series of different events, I ended up going to work with a church plant in Phnom Penh, Cambodia.

During my time in Cambodia I learned a number of things. Firstly, that my personality is not particularly suited to working full-time in a church. Secondly, that it is good to have a skill to offer if you are going to be in a developing world setting long-term. Thirdly, that poor physical health is hugely debilitating and also pervasive, limiting people's ability to work or to serve in/attend church. It angered me that so many of the girls in our congregation were paying money they did not have for very poor medical advice and intervention that they did not need, when much of their "illness" would have been cured by a better diet, and more education about healthy living. The problem was I was not qualified to give them the advice they needed.

I came back to the UK wondering if studying medicine was the way forward. It would be a huge time and financial investment, and would delay returning to Asia by several years, but it would help me to serve there in a practical and sustainable way. It seemed a bit faithless – should I not just go and preach the gospel and trust God with the rest? I applied anyway, reasoning that it was hard enough to become a doctor that there would be plenty of opportunity for God to stop me if it was a waste of time.

After two years of working to earn some money, then four long years of studying, by the grace of God, I graduated again. I then moved to London to start work. I wanted to be somewhere more ethnically diverse than where I had studied, and I wanted to serve a socially deprived population in preparation for moving back out to East Asia. I definitely got more than I bargained for!

There are a thousand things that I love about my job and I am so grateful to God for the privilege of doing something that genuinely uses all of me. However, over the last two years as a junior doctor there have been many ways in which my Christian integrity has been challenged and my original purpose for getting into medicine (to make Jesus known) has lost focus.

It is fair to say that the last two years of working have contained some of the most difficult experiences of my life. Things go wrong, often. Sometimes you feel directly responsible. There is nothing worse than feeling that you have caused someone harm because you forgot to do something, you could not be bothered to take the extra time to listen or you got a diagnosis or treatment wrong.

People are in their very worst state and families at their most stressed when they come into hospital. Long working hours can mean you can forget that anything good happens. Some weeks it feels like all you see is sickness, grief and death. It can be so all-consuming that I have often lost sight of why I became a doctor in the first place.

I have recently finished an A&E rotation, and ended up tired, bitter, and resentful of "time-wasters" – people who want a solution to a problem that medicine does not understand and/or cannot fix. I hardened my heart to their pain, largely because a lot of the time I felt unable to help. None of those attitudes particularly please God. To be a child of my Father in heaven means to be gracious, compassionate, and kind, demonstrating my Father's love, regardless of who they are (see Matthew 5:45). My own inability to do that is daily apparent; I am learning to ask the Holy Spirit to give me grace.

It is also humbling and a huge relief to remember that God is sovereign. Talking about church planting, Paul says, 'I planted the seed, Apollos watered it, but God made it grow. So neither he who plants nor he who waters are anything, but only God, who makes things grow' (see 1 Corinthians 3:6-7). Medicine is similar; I strongly believe that it is a good, and God-given, means of grace to us, but ultimately God is the One who heals – not our skill, or the sophistication of our science.

This means I can have peace as I can leave people in His hands. I do my best, but I know I am not ultimately responsible for whether someone lives or dies. He can heal, even when I mess up. As I (very) slowly learn to pray for my patients and to consciously acknowledge His work, His peace replaces the overwhelming anxiety that comes from inappropriate (and proud) assumptions of responsibility.

The medical world is very competitive, and you have to re-apply for jobs every couple of years. Success is measured by the training programme you are on, the number of publications you have, or the prestige of the hospital you work at.

It is easy to get swept up in all this and I have frequently lost sight of the fact that I started medicine in order to serve God in East Asia and to take the good news to those who have never heard it.

By His grace I am hoping to go back this summer, better qualified than I was before, but definitely no less dependent on Him.

Being a witness for Christ
in the world of contemporary art

Occupation: Visual Artist

This testimony focuses on my time studying for a master's degree at a well-known London art school. I would like to share three lessons that God taught me about how to be an effective witness to Christ in this context.

Being in community while on mission
During the summer before my course started, I found out that a friend who is also a Christian had got into the same college. This was helpful in a few different ways.

Firstly, when the subject of God came up in conversation with our course mates, it was harder to go quiet. Sometimes this was because we felt encouraged by the presence of the other. At other times, it was because we knew that the other would call us out if we let an opportunity slip past. Either way, the gospel was preached.

Secondly, we were able to sharpen each other's minds. The prevailing worldview in contemporary art is that truth is relative. With enough time spent immersed in this context, even the strongest Christian can let the sharpness of the gospel become dull. Several times my friend and I prayerfully weighed up things that had been said over us or over our work. With so many different relativist voices around us, we needed each other to set our minds back onto Jesus.

Finally, my friend and I were able to partner together in prayer and mission. Early on in the course, we made the decision to walk to the studio together once a week and pray for our course mates. One thing God put on our hearts was for there to be a change in the tone of our weekly group critiques. Initially, these were consumed with bitterness and ego. However, the more we prayed, the more we began to see a change. A year later and the tone was completely different. Critiques were now characterised by generosity and laughter. This was so obviously a work of God.

Filled with faith, my friend and I started to think in terms of introducing a "culture of honour", in which we would witness by living out a God-centred way of doing relationships. Christmas presented a great opportunity for this, and we decided to organise a bring-and-share dinner for our whole studio. Amazingly, we were able to hold it in a church building. On the day of the dinner we arranged the tables to surround a small wooden manger that the church had set out. Jesus was visibly at the centre of things.

Remaining in God's love
During my time studying, I found that telling my course mates about Jesus was much easier when I was actively enjoying His love. Jesus said in Matthew 12 that 'Out of the overflow of the heart, the mouth speaks.'

One afternoon, during a gallery visit with my tutorial group, God showed me how this relationship between my heart and my mouth could work to His glory. Looking around the collection of paintings at the Courtauld Institute, I stopped in front of *The Incredulity of Saint Thomas* by Caravaggio. The Holy Spirit came upon me as I stared at the image of the disciple greeting the risen Jesus. I was planted to the spot for what felt like an eternity.

After a while, my tutor came and stood beside me and I started telling her about why I found the work so affecting. It felt natural to talk about my relationship with Jesus and share with her that I was a "doubting Thomas" before encountering God in a personal way. She listened to everything I said and, to my surprise, invited me to tell the whole group about my experience later in the day!

It felt incredible to speak from the heart about Jesus in front of all my course mates. I know this was all because I took time to enjoy Him, rather than getting wrapped up in analysing my evangelistic strategy.

Remembering God goes before us
Another lesson that God taught me while at art school is that He goes before us in the harvest field. Sometimes I assume that every non-believer I speak to is either indifferent or dead set against God. The reality is often quite different.

Many people are already aware of Him or wrestling with spiritual issues even though they would not call themselves Christian. This hit home to me when, about a year into the course, I realised that nearly everyone in my studio had a church background to some degree! I was amazed to see that some of them were even articulating their spiritual hunger through their work.

On one occasion, a girl from my tutor group described her practice in terms of searching for holiness and purity. She boldly declared, 'Who gets to decide what is sacred and what is profane?'

Another time, a friend from the studio gave a presentation about the practice of confession in relation to art history. Afterwards I spoke with him about how Jesus is the atonement for our sin and, amazingly, he agreed to come to a Good Friday church service.

This hunger for God is not exclusive to art school. It extends into the world of contemporary art. Recently, a Turner Prize-winning artist came to give a lecture to us. While speaking about his work, he said in very plain terms, 'I want to have intimacy with something greater than myself.' This is a clear sign that God is at work in the world of visual art. It is also the reason why I, along with many other Christian artists, am committed to being faithfully present, in the hope that we will see a great kingdom harvest.

Flexible working
and the building of God's kingdom

Occupation: Private Tutor and Church Elder

Everyone in my family is hardworking and I am grateful for the pattern they set in working with integrity, diligence and stability. My father is an engineer and my mother is an accountant. Despite their experience and example, it took me several years to understand that work could actually be a part of God's plan for my life.

At the start of university I was at a spiritually critical moment. I was leading a fairly apathetic lifestyle, void of any real purpose or direction. I have been described as a "hopeless optimistic" on more than one occasion, and at that point in my life it was probably true.

However, God had plans afoot. My first week at university was the first week of a new church plant. I attended a meeting during Freshers' Week and noticed that I was the only one under thirty. During the ensuing months I realised God was about a greater purpose in my life, as He had surrounded me with people much more mature in their faith. My passion for the church grew and grew, and all other priorities seemed to fall into the background (including the idea of work). I passionately believed (and still do) in investing in the local church. I saw my time at university as a training ground for future church planting, and I am now in North London having helped to plant Revelation Church.

My attitude to work was one of "suffer it to survive" and then get on with the real business of building the church. I saw very little synergy between the two. I was never career-orientated and was often put off by people who were. I saw them as intense workaholics with little social life and no time for the church. I believed, whether vocally or by my actions, that it was "less spiritual".

So why does my story fit in a series of testimonies about work? Well, part of God's grace to me was my wife, who was more career-focused, but still held similar values about church and faith, although with a very different approach to living that out. I began to understand that a career is less about nine-to-five and more about vocation - vocation being the call that God has given you to be effective where he has placed you.

My vocation, as I understand it at this moment, is to build the church and effect change for the kingdom of God in North London. Therefore, for me, work always has to fit around church life rather than the other way round.

I am currently self-employed as a private tutor, working one-on-one with students. I therefore have the privilege of setting my own schedule. It gives me scope to prioritise midweek meetings, allowing flexibility for pastoral meetings and half/full days with the elders, as well as days away for conferences and the like.

There are many benefits to my work pattern but it is not without its challenges, including juggling church commitments with client demands, advanced diary planning, late night working and being clear on where my value comes from.

Church commitments versus client demands
Honouring God above man is a principle I hold dear (see Galatians 1:10). This gives immense freedom to value all relationships both at church and at work.

I try to live out James 5:12, 'Let your "yes" be yes and your "no" be no, so that you may not fall under condemnation.' This way I can provide an example for many who are not believers. There are occasionally mistakes, either by myself or administratively. In these instances I have to weigh up the factors and decide in conjunction with the company I work for what to do and figure out how best to serve all parties. I also recognise that a big part of my industry is building a reputation as being reliable and consistent in the standard of service I deliver. This has, on occasion, although rarely, led to me working on a Sunday, something I fight to avoid in order to prioritise church meetings and family.

Diary planning and lead times

The nature of tutoring is that parents book lessons in your diary months in advance, often about six to nine months in advance. This is really tricky as it means having to plan ahead, with an idea of where I will be and what I will be invested in at that time. As such, my wife and I try to set our holiday schedule about a year in advance, so we have time booked out for family.

Advanced planning can feel uncomfortable for many people. Today's culture encourages us not to commit and to keep our options open. However, if we are to be effective in work or even at church, planning ahead is something we need to engage with and get better at.

The obvious question is then, what happens when dates change? Sometimes it is possible to juggle things around, if you know what your commitments are and what time you have available. This is only possible with an up-to-date diary. Sometimes, though, it will mean missing out on certain events. Recently the date of a church leaders' day was changed. As one of the elders, together with the team, we had to make a call. We moved the date and I did not attend. On these rare occasions I feed in my thoughts and prayers prior to the event.

Late working and unsociable hours

I often work very late into the evening because that is one of the preferred times for tutorials. This makes things tricky for getting home to look after my daughter but it does mean that I usually then have time during the day for other commitments. To prioritise family I also take every Thursday off to look after her knowing that most Saturdays I will be indisposed.

The hardest part of this is then finding time with my wife. We often touch base only briefly face-to-face during the week. This has meant that we have to work hard at making contact throughout the working day, to draw each other into our respective lives and situations. We try to speak two or three times a day, sometimes more if there are pressing things to address.

Being clear on where my value comes from

As a consultant on an hourly rate it can be easy to attribute my time to the value that people will pay. I have never been particularly ambitious or had a great desire to earn a lot of money. I have often felt it carries too much responsibility for me to handle, cautious of the call in Luke 12:48. However, as my hourly rates have increased, I have had to keep myself in check, not to value myself by the rates I charge.

Additionally, because my pay is quite literally linked to the amount I work, I have had to be careful not to work unsustainable hours just to earn more. When working out whether to take on a new student I try not to think about it in terms of how much the client is paying. I think in terms of whether it will practically fit in my schedule.

I track my pay for invoicing and tax returns, but philosophically I consider my pay to come from God. If God is my Provider, then I can have absolute confidence that He knows what I need. If my remuneration increases, it says more about what God is calling me to steward than how valued I am.

Let me leave you with the call from Colossians 3:23. We work for the Lord and that goes for every area of our lives: work, home and church. I believe work is broader than just what I get paid for; it encompasses all I am invested in. This does blur the lines somewhat but if we keep our eyes on God as our true employer He gives grace and capacity for all He puts in our job description.

Work and family

Two careers, one marriage and being united on one journey

Occupation: Teacher (husband) and Financial Services Regulator (wife)

Looking back over the past eight years, a significant area in which we have seen the faithfulness of God and learned to trust Him – His guidance, His timing, His direction – is with our jobs, in particular learning how to pursue our careers separately but together, and always before God, as part of our marriage.

Among many others, there are probably three key examples from our lives where this has been true.

Our road trip to Washington DC (from the wife's perspective)

Several years ago I was offered an opportunity to work for six months in Washington, DC. Going on an external secondment was a part of the graduate development programme I was on, but the placement in DC was particularly attractive. It was offered as a strategic secondment to help build links between the US and UK organisations, and the timing meant it would be a great opportunity to learn about post-financial crisis reforms in the US, both of which would be valuable experiences.

However, on the face of it, spending six months in another country without a clear purpose made little sense to my husband. It meant giving up his job and, although the fact that he was at a crossroads in his work meant this was not a very difficult choice, taking himself out of work and having a gap on his CV so early on in his career meant that this was not totally straightforward. It also meant leaving his life and friends in the UK for a time, to prioritise my job.

However, we felt that it was important for our relationship that we should both go. Throughout our three years of marriage leading up to this point, I had been commuting three hours a day on top of a busy job, whereas my husband was doing a job that did not present many opportunities to progress. We agreed that spending the time apart would not do anything to strengthen our marriage, but the solution was not for me to pull back in my job.

So we went to DC. My husband found a distance-learning course (he did not have a visa, so could not work or study), and we both made friends through a local church and my work. We found that it was a fantastic time for us as a couple: we had lots of fun, and though of course I was working, we were able to use the time as a "break"; being out of our usual environment meant we were able to grow closer together.

As for my husband's job, towards the end of our time in DC, we were praying together as we walked around the Capitol building one evening, and I felt very clearly that God was going to place him in a job that he would absolutely love and in which he would grow. And, though the direction was not what we expected, He did.

In choosing to prioritise my job over his – even if at first glance (for me at least!) it seemed like a no-brainer – we found that it was important to take a broader perspective, prayerfully considering together the wider implications, for him and also for our marriage, of the decision we were taking. This time was significant for my job, but looking back, it was even more important for strengthening our marriage.

A new direction into teaching (from the husband's perspective)
More recently, I was encouraged to train to become a teacher by a Head of Department in the school in which I was working as a cover supervisor. I had taken this job as a stopgap while working out what I wanted to do longer-term, having left teacher training once before and being determined not to stay in education. With this background, I was initially very sceptical,

but over time became more and more certain that this was a good step for me to take, and that the factors that had prompted my previous decision no longer applied.

For my wife, however, this decision meant losing my salary for a year and for me to pursue something I had already stopped doing once before. As she began to pray about the decision, individually and with me, it became crystal clear that she needed to trust God with our future, and importantly, fully support me with my decision no matter what happened.

As we prayed, we felt prompted to ask God to provide financially, specifically asking that He would cover my salary. There was no prospect of this happening, but after I was accepted onto the training programme, two things happened which meant that our income increased by as much as my previous salary. More importantly, through this and the following year of my training, my wife learned to trust God with my career, and our security, more than she had previously done.

We have learned that God's provision for us is so much bigger than our pay cheques, and we must not look to our jobs for security, but rather to Him, as everything we have is from Him. We need to follow Him faithfully and trust His prompting.

Supporting each other (from the husband's perspective)
There have been several occasions in which one or the other of us has had an opportunity to go for a new job, or something in one of our jobs has been especially difficult. In the early days, it is probably fair to say that we dealt with these instances almost independently of each other, as the individual's responsibility.

However, over the years, as with other things in our marriage, we have learned to bring these to God together. It has been a joy to learn to carry these things together, and we have learned to support one another, even when (perhaps *particularly* when) there is some sacrifice involved.

When my wife had the opportunity to go for a great job that would involve longer hours, we prayerfully made the decision together, and I supported her throughout the two-plus years she was doing that job. This often involved doing more than my share of the cooking on workday evenings!

In another situation, when I was applying for jobs a year ago, my wife was praying and felt prompted to encourage me on a particular evening when I was feeling discouraged, to look for relevant jobs available that day, and to apply. I acted on this encouragement immediately, submitting an application and notifying my employer that evening. God worked through that to bless me with not one but two job offers within a week – not only providing a job that gave me everything I was looking for, but also encouraging me to trust Him, and using the situation to show us again that He will provide for us.

We are learning to always pray together about decisions affecting each other's work. With this consistent inclusion of each other and God in our approach to our jobs, we have found that we are stronger and more effective, both at work, and in our marriage.

Responding to unexpected circumstances by faith: home educating my children

Occupation: Home Educator

I never, not once, when thinking about becoming a mum, considered home educating my children. Even after having children, our conviction was that I would nurture our children until they reached school age. They would then go to school and I would return to a normal paid job.

We have three children. Our first two went to school. Even when my third child was one, I was already thinking about going back to work so that we could have two incomes. After six years being a full-time mum and my third child not long due in nursery, I had already started working part-time from home to engage myself with being employed. I have a high capacity, love studying and am very task-focused, so the prospect of going back to full-time employment excited me.

However, one of our children had some difficult experiences at school. These very quickly led to our decision to home educate, mainly because the alternatives were genuinely no better. This unexpected circumstance raised three key issues that I needed to work through.

Firstly, I had to face the fear that I would fail at home educating my children. Secondly, I had to lay down the desires, visions and dreams I had for going back to full-time employment and the career development that provided.

Finally, I was finding it difficult to not be contributing to our family finances. Raising a family near central London is expensive and we have had to keep a tight budget.

I recognised that I could not ignore these issues as I embarked upon this new challenge. In order to respond to this new role well I needed to acknowledge the reality of the situation and most importantly welcome God to soften my heart on a daily basis so that I learned to trust Him. This way I would not leave any room for fear and bitterness to creep in. I wanted to be able to rely on God for His grace to do what was needed.

Our Father is so good. He leads us by still waters and restores our soul. He gives us peace and makes right what is in us as we abide in Him (see Psalm 23). As such, I was able to lay down the second and third issue and give them to God with confidence in my heart. He has changed my vision for the present and given me faith that, in the grand scheme of things, home educating my children will not take much time out of my dreams and desires for other jobs. I have realised that His thoughts are so much higher than mine and I am excited by that. He is teaching me what kingdom ambition is as I seek first His kingdom and righteousness (see Matthew 6:33).

During this period, one key question I have faced is the extent to which I live to honour God and be pleasing to Him, or in fear of what people think of me as being *just* a mum. However, I have come to the conclusion that to be a full-time mum and educate my children, by using all the skills, gifts and creativity that I have, is an honour. To serve God in this way is to be my ambition and worship to him.

On the third point then: God continues to provide for us more than we can imagine. There have been many answered prayers, and they have blown us away. I am constantly and encouragingly reminded of who He is and what He has done and this fuels my faith, especially when I am tempted to believe the lies that what I am doing is useless and a waste of time.

The benefit that the boys have experienced is obvious; they are growing in peace and confidence and just simply loving life and learning.

My fear of failing at home educating took a bit more time to become free from. I recognised after a while that the initial fear was more a concern that I would not be able to teach the kids well (at least in comparison to a school system that has been thought out by many skilled and experienced people). However, this healthy emotion meant I cared and I was able to engage with how to develop the right materials, resources, style and structure to teach my children well.

God also pointed out to me that this could be a fear that developed and controlled my motivations if I did not understand that it is not about me getting things perfect. It is, nonetheless, about being able to respond to what is needed in faith, having a go at things and being OK with failing. If one style does not work, then we can try another. If I make mistakes, then I say sorry and we move on. He will provide all the strength, creativity and patience I need as I look to Him.

Another revelation was that while we thought our decision to home educate was based on the lack of school spaces (we explored many alternatives to the school my son was in before turning to home schooling), God has shown us that He had another, wider and deeper perspective on the situation.

God has since spoken to us about returning home to the Middle East, where my husband and I are from. This is where we now want to live and make disciples. God knew, when we did not, that home educating our children would provide the time and space to plan for this transition. In addition, it has also made the adjustment much easier as we will, more than likely, home educate our children, at least initially after arriving there. Our children are already settled into the rhythm of learning at home, which will minimise big changes in the first few months. Also, being free from the constraints of the conventional school term has enabled us to attend conferences as a family (during school term time) to plan and equip us for this move.

God is always teaching us how to live for Him and His purposes. Paul urges us in his letter to the Romans to present our bodies as a living sacrifice, holy and acceptable to God, which is our spiritual worship (see Romans 12:1). My life is in Christ, so my whole life belongs to God.

In His mercy and by His grace He is teaching me how to adore and praise Him with my life choices and the way I live. I have made sacrifices in order to home educate my children, and I do not always enjoy it, but He has shown me that this is to make me more Christ-like in my character and help me grow in faith.

The joy in this new season has been deeper than I imagined and it is so good to be where He wants me. I feel like I have developed and grown more in my role as a full-time, home educating mum than any other role I could have been in.

When we are obedient to Him, we are like the branches with Jesus as our vine (see John 15:1-17). We become fruitful in what we do and He prunes the branches that are not of Him. He has pruned in me the fear of failure and the wrong ambitions and motives. In His mercy God has developed in me faith for all that He can do as I live in obedience to Him and look to see my life from His perspective.

Things do not always go to plan

Occupation: Product Manager for a major online retailer

Ever since I can remember, I have been ambitious. Growing up, I loved learning and had a good head for numbers, but was easily bored. Uninterested in day-to-day goings-on, my teenage conversations would often veer towards future career aspirations (barrister, chemistry professor, etc.) and which university would best facilitate achieving those dreams.

As I got a bit older and became more established in my Christian faith (I grew up in church), I understood these character traits to be how God had made me and that I was to make the most of the gifts and personality He had given me. Even more so, I wanted to really go for it in life. I thought this looked like going to the best university, getting the best job and getting to the top of that field in order to have an influence there for God.

At university, as well as my growing love for and knowledge of God, my ambitions swelled. I was in a good church that encouraged Christians to see life's work as transforming *everything*, with a focus on evangelism and bettering our surroundings by bringing God's perspective into the day-to-day. There was a clear emphasis on an outward-looking life with a missional focus and a "you can do anything" culture. I took this challenge seriously but simplistically, confirming my original ambitions that I would get a "highflyer" job, live in London until at least middle age, be promoted quickly through the ranks to get to an influential position and probably be single for quite a while as I put my hand to the City job plough.

My plans were scuppered by the credit crunch. The investment bank I worked in during summer 2008 lost close to £40bn in the sub-prime crisis and so what should have been a watertight way of getting a banking graduate job did not present the opportunity I expected. I turned to Teach First, finished the two years with them and, once the credit crunch dust had settled, I decided strategy consulting was for me.

I accepted a job working for a great firm and expected to work there, stay single and become a partner. However, a month after accepting the offer, one of my friends became something more and soon we were married. Being a married strategy consultant was challenging. I had expected to be single, with free evenings to spend working the extra hours needed to get promoted quickly. Being married was such a blessing, but balancing marriage and the "work hard, play hard" culture at work was tricky and my younger colleagues thought it was totally weird. I battled with the temptation to think that the grass felt greener too – surely it was easier to work hard and get ahead without competing priorities.

Nevertheless, I managed to join in, and I did quite well. I never had that Sunday night feeling and was learning a lot. The job was intellectually stretching which I really enjoyed and I saw myself staying at the company for a long time. I could certainly see how God might use this job to propel me to a place of influence and I felt really called to that environment. I hardly ever saw my friends or my supportive husband, but I told myself this was God's calling so it was worth the sacrifice.

Around two years in, when I should have been gearing up for promotion, my husband started getting really down. We had recently decided he should quit his job working for a charity out of town and remove the commute by going self-employed. It was tough at first, and I was carrying the financial burden, which meant that my salary, rather than paying for amazing holidays and new clothes that my peers were enjoying, was paying the bills.

His decreasing mood and lack of energy meant I started carrying the emotional burden as well. I would be in the middle of a deal at work, when I would get a tearful call. I found it hard to detach myself and I felt torn and frustrated that I could not be in two places at once. I was also frustrated that I could not fix my husband's feelings, despite my many problem-solving attempts. None of my ideas seemed to work. I also allowed selfish thoughts to fester, of him holding me back from my "true calling" and success. It was exhausting trying to keep his mood up all the time and think of ways to help him feel better.

I was not very good at putting on a "game face" at work. I was too distracted to concentrate on mentally stretching work, and I found myself in a downward spiral of less-than-perfect performance and dented confidence, tying myself in knots. While my husband's condition improved, my knocked confidence lingered and I found it hard to get back into the groove. This was exacerbated because I was in a workplace where not showing emotion was admired and also because I felt like I was letting God down on what He had called me to. I was not only performing below my expectations and those of the firm, but the *meaning* of not performing well was crushing me.

My husband and I decided more structured employment might be better for him, to both financially provide and keep up his mood. He landed a job in a school as a sports assistant – it really felt like God's provision. However, as things started looking up and I began to get back on my feet, my husband went the other way. Rather than being low and unmotivated suddenly he was frantic, talking at me for forty-five minutes without stopping, buying new things for himself as soon as a new client had paid him and he seemed gradually more intense and unhinged. The behaviour was very confusing and for a while it felt like I was married to a different person. As the behaviour got stranger, my work was further affected as my mind felt overwhelmed, and this was all happening when I was hoping to be promoted. Nothing was going to plan.

Then my husband was fired from a job that I had viewed as God's provision for us, and this triggered a series of more serious conversations with a psychiatrist. My firm did not promote me and they made it clear they were not prepared to accommodate my situation given how it was affecting my performance.

After a few weeks of care from a mental health crisis team my husband was diagnosed with Type 1 Bipolar Disorder and I realised this would have consequences beyond the immediate weeks. It would mean that, while I could try to regain my reputation at work, the likelihood was that I would be needed at home far more and simply would not have the emotional resilience or capacity to make that happen.

Rather embarrassed and with confidence dented further, I realised I needed to look for another job. I had to give back to God what I felt He had given me in the first place, which was quite painful. Gone were my aspirations of making partner and endless five-year plans. I had to look instead to today, no further ahead, and I also had to let go of the recent discouraging events. I had to trust God to uphold today's steps and "hern me in" (see Proverbs 19:21 and Psalm 139:5).

I looked hard at what "God's calling" meant, and realised I had become a sufferer of "individualitis", seeing life as primarily about achieving my own plans, even if I thought they were honouring God. I had become far too fixated on my own plans, and whether I considered the situation I was in to be impressive and ambitious enough to display God's "favour" on my career (as if that were the way God displayed His favour). God showed me that He had a much bigger plan, that I could not control everything and that He was looking for me to know Him more and align with His plan rather than simply execute my own.

I had to accept that this might be the end of my consulting career, reluctantly retiring early from something I enjoyed without much choice. While looking for a new job, by God's grace I landed a great role at a major online retailer, enabling me to keep learning and enjoying work but with a more flexible situation. This has enabled me to recover from being a carer — something that took longer than expected.

I have worked hard in this new job, but have chosen to put in boundaries and am now working fewer hours than before, even if that slows me down a bit career-wise. I have learned that I need to obey Him with what He has put in front of me, and then trust Him with the rest. Like most things I learned this the hard way!

Now on the other side, my husband is much better, although we have scaled back on a number of things to help avoid his health deteriorating again. We are learning how to walk this sometimes complicated and difficult journey, confident that His purposes are more glorious and far bigger than we could ask or imagine. Our hearts are softer and our egos are smaller. Funnily enough, I have never been rated as well on my performance and am about to move internally to an amazing new role.

As a couple we have a renewed focus on pursuing maturity and sharing the gospel. My husband's illness has even been helpful in our ability to support and disciple others, which has been a privilege to see. Work is still something I feel very called to. I want to work hard in places where Christians are few and where I can be involved in exciting things. It is no longer just my plan in the way I see it. Instead I am excited to see how God's story unfolds and the part that I can play in that.

Workplace blessing for Kingdom giving

Occupation: Financial Services Regulator
and stay-at-home mum

Our vision for our work is all about what our work, and succeeding at work, is able to achieve in our local community. In the Bible we are told to 'look after orphans and widows' (see James 1:27). We want to work hard in order to create ways we can do exactly this.

For us this means that we want to do work well so that one day we can own a large house, which then allows us to foster and adopt. We would love to host people who want to give their time to the church, or who cannot afford housing for a season. In order to do this in a really sustainable way we need space, and so our journey is very much about partnering with God to make this happen.

We are part of a local church that has a lot of people who are passionate about seeing God's kingdom come in our city. We are a demographically young church in a really expensive city and it is fair to say that there are not many people with big homes and spare rooms.

We look around us, at our situation and the situation of many others of a similar age, and there are two possible responses. One option is that we succumb to our lack of faith and jump online and start searching for jobs, probably somewhere in the north of England where houses are a fraction of the price they are in London, and people actually have gardens. While this is not wrong in itself, we recognise that for us this could be an escape from what God is doing where we live. The other response then is one of faith. This one involves complete dependence on God to make it happen.

The funny thing is, although the lack of faith response seems the realistic response to our situation, it really is not. Our faith-filled response is actually based on a greater reality, where God provides not only for our needs, but for our desires too (see Psalm 37:4). This has been our enduring experience.

When we got engaged, we were in debt and our prayer was, 'Lord, help us to enter marriage not in the negative.' We also decided to give away any money that we had in our bank account at the point of getting married (if there was anything). The single most important thing to do with our money was to *first* give back to God. Despite our desire to clear our debt and pay for our wedding, it was still so important to give from every bit of money that came in. This is in line with Proverbs 3:9 where is says, 'Honour the Lord with your wealth, with the *firstfruits* of all your crops.' Needless to say, we did not enter marriage in the negative. Somehow, we began with over one thousand pounds! We gave this away and in less than a month we got given an amount much larger than this.

Five months later we were renting a one-bedroom flat when we found out that my wife was pregnant. We were already at the limits of what we could afford on rent so our options felt limited. We started expecting God to show us where we should move (somewhere more affordable). However, He actually provided somewhere in the same borough. We got accepted for a two-bed, shared ownership property in Farringdon, and as we moved in, our expenses were less than our rental property.

At every stage we realised that God was not just meeting our needs, but *exceeding* our expectations. Without a shadow of a doubt we were seeing the reality of Luke 6:38 where it says:

> **'Give, and it will be given to you. A good measure, pressed down, shaken together and running over, will be poured into your lap. For with the measure you use, it will be measured to you.'**
> (Luke 6:38)

We have learned that we need not be scared to give, because He always meets and goes beyond our needs.

During this time, I had put in extra hours at work and hoped I would earn a big bonus at the end of the financial year. When bonus time came around, I received a basic bonus, and wondered if I really should have invested so many extra hours at work.

The following year, we had our daughter. I still worked hard, but family became a priority. At this time, when all of my fellow graduates were pouring in as much time at work as they could to progress, I was leaving at five and coming home to help my wife care for our child. Our little girl was not a good sleeper. We would frequently be awake for several hours in the middle of the night, trying to get her back to sleep. That year felt like it was about surviving, and yet when bonus time came around, I received double what I expected. We certainly felt like we were living according to God's economy, and not our own.

Further evidence of this was when I applied for another job. I did not feel qualified for this job but I got it. It did not seem to make sense, but then the second half of Proverbs 3:9-10 says, 'then your barns will be filled to overflowing, and your vats will brim over with new wine.' Not only had God given me a big bonus but also He had now given me a new job with a higher salary on top.

So now, when we look forward to our future plans – opening up our home and bringing children into our family – we know we must not put our limitations on what God can do. I must honour God in my workplace, and we must give back to Him what He has so generously given us.

We believe that our work helps facilitate bringing God's kingdom rule in our home, in church life and in our city. The more money we are able to earn, the more money we can give back to God, and the closer we come to owning a many-bedroomed house to use in response to God's call to love the orphan and the widow. We have faith that we will find favour with our bosses, colleagues, the housing market, and who knows who or what else. We have now begun expecting God's exciting interventions.

Work and
trusting God

Pursuing a career at the risk that it may not pay off

Occupation: Screenwriter

I graduated from university without any clear idea of what I wanted to do. I had grown up in a family where parents, siblings, cousins, etc. had gone into "proper" jobs and careers: lawyers, doctors, nurses, engineers and so on. Nothing of this nature really appealed to me and, at the time, it was hard to appreciate the full extent of the jobs that existed out in the real world. I also found it difficult to see past the rigidly academic expectations of my school and university.

I had always assumed that God would provide for me career-wise, but oddly that manifested as a reluctance to commit to anything specific. When leaving university, it can feel like one wrong move might put you on a permanently erroneous path. Looking back, this illustrates how small an opinion of God's sovereignty and provision I actually had. Thankfully, He is so gracious; He was willing to meet me where I was at and to spend the next few years gently leading me.

I guess this was the start of my moving from a head-knowledge of what God says in His word, to a life based on trusting those promises as real and life-giving. However, it was a long, arduous process, one in which the main obstacle was always me.

As I was finishing my studies, one of my friends asked if I would like to join him in attempting to become TV writers and to form a writing partnership. It sounded brilliant, tapping into my personality and the things I am good at. However, the reality is that many people dream of becoming a writer, but very few reach a level where they make a sustainable living. Practical considerations like income would become very real concerns. Having prayed about it, I decided to give it a go and test the water.

My now-wife and I became engaged soon after; someone else was now going to be caught up in the decision I had taken. She was completely supportive and encouraging, which released me to continue my move into this financially unstable industry.

We (my writing partner and I) soon hit a breakthrough in our work. It was an amazing moment, but one that marked the beginning of the real struggle. We now knew we had ability, but it meant we had to get down to the hard graft of realising that skill. It was time either to commit fully by choosing to abandon the idea of pursuing a "normal" career, or to step back from writing completely. I sought much counsel from wise Christians who walk closely with God, prayed, and felt that God was giving me the freedom to dive headfirst into this world if I wanted to.

This initial success soon led to another major milestone, one which genuinely left me thinking I would be a millionaire within six months: we sold an idea to a major production company.

A year later, I had made a few hundred pounds.

This was to be the basic pattern for the following six years: significant projects put into development that showed great promise but never quite made it. Each one felt like it might just get there; each one would get a little further down the development path than the last – a pilot episode written, or a script making it to the top of a broadcaster's commissioning pile – but each one would eventually hit an impasse and get turned down. In the world of screenwriting, most of the money comes at the back end of the development lifecycle. If a project fails to get to screen, you are unlikely to make much money.

Every time I would be devastated, and every time my wife and I would pray, seek God's will, and feel like it was right for me to continue. I did various part-time jobs to try to supplement her income (she was supporting both of us) but writing remained what I felt called to.

Then, seven years after I started, God opened the floodgates. We have more work than we can handle and have had to start turning things down.

Now, it has to be said, all that I have just written is filtered through the fine lens of hindsight. I have looked back over my career so far and I have placed a narrative of God's provision upon it, not because it was not there at the time, but because in the midst of it, I could not see it.

God is good and His word is true. He makes paths straight (see Proverbs 3:6) and works things for the good of those that love Him (see Romans 8:28). A huge part of this is handing our own personal dreams over to God, trusting that He will make them exactly what we *need* (not want). There is nothing that will make us more fulfilled, content, and joyous than that.

I say this because I have a real distaste for testimonies that make out like the writer was sure of this in every moment or acts as though, even in the tough times, they were fully certain that they were following God's will. In so, so, *so* many moments, I was not. I raged against God at yet another set back, tried to blackmail God with, 'if this project does not come through, I am throwing in the towel!' I ranted at friends and my wife, using them as proxies for what I wanted God to hear just in case He had not noticed me speaking to Him directly; not exactly noble or virtuous moments.

People would compliment me on my trust in God by running this hard route, and I would thank them, deflecting their comments upwards with fixed-smile platitudes about God's provision, while inside still hoping for the moment my career hit the big time and people would be amazed with me as a person, and what I had achieved. Thankfully, those seven years allowed God to gently humble me.

Finally, those straight paths and the good things that God promises to those who love Him are almost guaranteed not to look how we expect or want them to look. When you are in the middle of a terribly dark moment, when all things seem to be crashing down around you, the imaginary, sun-dappled path you probably pictured seems more like a storm-lashed mountain pass. It is in these moments that God is revealed as the only solid rock, the true foundation we ought to build our lives on. If He were to call me to put my career down, He would give me the grace to be at peace with that.

If there is anything about my testimony that is impressive, it is God Himself. The fact that He cares about our struggles is amazing; the fact that He wants us to see them as nothing in comparison to knowing and following Him is even more mind-blowing. It looks like madness to the world, but it is where peace and fulfillment lie.

God's plan, God's timing

Occupation: Senior Executive for a global music exam board

I have always been ambitious. At school I always wanted to get the highest marks in the class and at work I constantly strive for the highest levels of performance. God has given me huge favour in the workplace but I still rely far too heavily on my own efforts in order to make things happen. This has often taken the place of trusting Him.

Since completing my degree in music, I have worked for just one company. As the leading music exam board globally, being offered a job with this organisation, straight out of university, was like striking gold. I had done all of the piano grades through this board during my school years and here I was, all these years later, as an employee – thank you Lord!

I received a promotion within eighteen months to a new role, looking after the administration across a suite of countries. With this promotion came increased responsibility but I was ready for it and I felt that God was definitely in it.

After a further eight months, our department had a restructure and I was promoted to my current position, looking after the company's work in some of our most significant overseas markets. This role came with international travel and responsibility for multi-million pound operating budgets. I was now visiting some of the most fascinating places across South East Asia, staying in top hotels, eating amazing food and meeting with music teachers, studio owners and government officials in all these places. I remember giving a testimony in church about how much favour God had given me and how none of this would have happened otherwise, although inwardly I suppose I was still proud of myself and what I felt were my own achievements.

As I developed within the role, I quickly became frustrated by the lack of opportunity to progress further within the company. As a medium-sized charity, promotions are really only available when someone leaves or there is a restructure. As a result I began looking at other people around me – notably friends from church – who seemed to have progressed to more senior roles with higher salaries. It was at this point that I started looking at what else I could do. Surely, I thought, with several years of solid experience, international travel and a can-do attitude, I should be able to get a job elsewhere that would elevate my status and pay packet!

Working for a charity can be very rewarding but the salary levels are much more modest compared with similar roles in other sectors. I started looking at consulting opportunities in major firms, reasoning that I had a transferable skill-set and would be able to fast-track my way to management level and earn much more. This was also necessary, I told myself, as we had recently bought a flat in London and had a mortgage to pay.

Instead of fast-tracking my way to greater success, God showed me that I was fast-tracking my way to idolatry.

During the first instalment of a workplace series, run by my local church and given by a retired senior partner in the world of consulting, I felt God speak to me clearly about staying put. My search for more responsibility and a higher salary was not primarily a desire for more money, but for greater status. I wanted to be seen as a high achiever by my friends and family. I wanted to be seen as having a level of influence and responsibility within the workplace that was greater than others had. I wanted to set myself apart from others.

My wife had been partnering with me in these struggles throughout, but after God spoke to me about this covetousness we knew we needed to pursue Him more in prayer, both together and within our accountability groups at church.

Why had God wanted me to stay put? God wanted me in this organisation and He had called me to work within the music education sector. The work was not done. He had given me influence and fantastic contacts within music education and the only thing that had changed was that I had become greedy!

God has been gracious and patient throughout my journey and I have a newfound trust in Him. I am confident that His plans are good and His timing is perfect. Jeremiah 29:11 has been spoken over me in recent years and is confirmation that God's purposes are good:

'For I know the plans I have for you,' declares the Lord, 'plans to prosper you and not to harm you, plans to give you hope and a future.' (Jeremiah 29:11)

I have learned that we need to put our trust in God each and every day. Romans 8:28 says, 'that in all things God works for the good of those who love Him, who have been called according to His purpose.' It is really important to hold onto this truth and to seek God in prayer and worship, otherwise we can fall back into relying on our own strength and our own plans.

While we may think our plans are good, God's plans are perfect and trustworthy. I have also learned that God has incredible amounts of patience with us!

My prayer is that this testimony offers encouragement to you and that God speaks, guides, renews and blesses you in your own journey, just as He has in mine.

Having confidence to trust God for where He has you

Occupation: Business Development Manager for a care and support provider

Learning to trust God
Towards the end of my degree, I knew that God wanted me to stay in Camden, to be part of a local church there, so I prayed for work. God provided for me very quickly as I was offered a job just one week after I finished university.

After a year in the workplace, I started a graduate scheme in a care and support organisation. I found out my first placement was working in a men's hostel with vulnerable individuals, including those with substance misuse needs and offending histories.

This was not what I had in mind at all. I questioned why God would place me there particularly when He knew that I had some recent negative experiences with men including being followed and having my bag stolen by a young male. I was so keen to be successful on the graduate scheme that I did not raise these concerns with my workplace and I thought I would give it a go.

While working there I witnessed conflict and experienced aggression most weeks. I found this very intimidating and some days, particularly when I was on late shifts, I really dreaded going to work. I felt very dependent on God for my safety. I would often pray for God's protection as I walked around the hostel.

During one particularly challenging shift we called the police because a former resident who was a member of a gang returned to the hostel and was behaving aggressively towards staff. At this point even friends and family thought I should resign. Fortunately I had a holiday booked the next week. It was perfect timing. God used the week away to strengthen me. I decided to stay and prayed a lot more!

God was not only teaching me how to trust Him to look after me, but after a while I started to realise that God had placed me there as part of His redemptive plan. One of the privileges of this job was hearing the stories of the men I was supporting. Most of the men I was working with had faced trauma and great adversity; many felt hopeless after years of substance misuse and/or homelessness. Through revealing their brokenness God was challenging my perceptions of not only the men I worked with but also those in my community.

I would frequently reflect on the parallels with the gospel, recognising my own brokenness, and God's consistency towards me. God was beginning to cultivate in me a heart of compassion towards men, particularly with complex needs, rather than fear and judgement. I had expected to get many things out of the graduate scheme but this certainly was not what I had anticipated.

Finding security regardless of success or failure
My next challenge in learning to trust God was in a completely different environment. As part of the graduate scheme I was given the opportunity to work in the business development team. I found myself working in a competitive, performance-driven culture, where success was measured by winning contracts.

It was a steep learning curve gaining the skills required for this new role. At times I felt discouraged and insecure as I did not feel I was contributing to the team in the way that I wanted to or that I thought I should.

A few months in my mum gave me a prophetic word about being promoted within the team. Foolishly I laughed and stated that I struggled to see how that was going to happen. I was finding the job I had difficult enough!

God had other plans. After nine months, I applied for, and was given, the promotion within the team.

Despite the fact that I knew God had given me this new role I still felt insecure and inadequate. Taking a significant step up in responsibility within a relatively short timeframe was challenging. I transitioned, almost overnight, from being "good" at my role to being completely "out of my depth".

I was on annual leave on my first day in the new role because I was attending a Christian leadership conference held in Westminster City Hall, just a few minutes from my workplace. What timing! It was amazing to think that in my first week God had taken me out of work to equip me for my new role, for being a leader in my workplace and for stewarding the blessing that He had given me. What provision!

At the conference someone prayed for me about leadership and God providing me with an opportunity. By the time I returned to work I felt further assured that it was God who had given me the position and that it was God who would also enable me to do my job well.

One particularly challenging week involved working to a deadline with only half a team. I was on the Victoria Line (on my way to work), praying desperately, and God gave me the following encouragement: although God is calling us into perfection, through Jesus and His redemptive work, He sees our heart in our work. I felt reassured that God values my work and efforts, even if the results were not as I had wanted them to be. God is much more concerned with whether we are motivated by a love for Him than exactly what we are producing or the technical expertise we have.

Remaining to grow

The significant reduction in local authority budgets over the last few years has increased competition within the care, support and housing sectors, making it more difficult to win contracts and reach financial targets.

It can be quite demoralising at times, particularly when you take personal responsibility. I find it tempting to entertain thoughts of leaving when things get tough.

Earlier this year I was offered a job, with higher pay and less pressure. It was so tempting to take it. I prayed about it but God told me He was not finished yet. I know God does not want me to run from a challenging job or sector; in fact God wants me to embrace the adventure of learning to trust Him and depend on His strength. I have learned that when we are out of our depth, our potential for growth increases.

In both my successes and failures I have had to find my security in God and not in my own performance. I am learning that God is so gracious towards us, bearing with us when we fail, supporting us as we learn but also delighting with us when we succeed.

My best days are when I let Him take control, not trying to prove myself. I find on these occasions that I can really invest in developing others, valuing and recognising their contribution.

The following verses in Proverbs 3 have been a reminder for me to focus on loving God and people and to trust that His favour will follow:

> **'Let not steadfast love and faithfulness forsake you; bind them around your neck; write them on the tablet of your heart. So you will find favour and good success in the sight of God and man.'** (Proverbs 3:3-4)

Godly commitment to and passion for your work against all odds

Occupation: Composer

I discovered the joys of playing music when I was twelve years old. As soon as I started, I knew it was what I wanted to do when I was older. From the day that my dad taught me my first piano chords I was writing songs.

At fifteen I heard God speak to me about doing music as a career and by the time I was eighteen I had many separate prophetic words confirming this. I finished my A Levels and moved up to Camden, North London. I was confident that God had led me down this path and I was confident, maybe even slightly arrogant, in my musical ability.

I spent the next three years leading music in church and playing gigs outside of church. At twenty-two, I got married and my wife and I both felt God was calling me to take a step of faith and go full-time as a musician/songwriter.

It never occurred to me that I might not be successful. This was not because of a confidence in myself but because God had asked me to do it. However, over the next year I had door after door of opportunities close on me. I struggled to get any meaningful work. The hard thing was that I always got down to the last two of an audition or would get the job and then the whole thing would collapse before it got going.

I took every opportunity seriously and worked as hard as I could to get every job that came up but it never happened. I tried to be faithful with the little and give my all to anything God gave me. I remember getting a call on a Friday about a job and working all weekend to prepare for the audition. I even did a twelve-hour day on the bank holiday Monday while all my friends were out having fun. I did not get the job but I know that my efforts did not go unnoticed by Him.

This was really hard in the first year of marriage, particularly because I felt the pressure of wanting to be a husband that provided for his wife. I had friends who did not understand and thought that I was just being lazy and needed to grow up and get a proper career. I felt let down by God. I had really held onto Scripture, of victory and provision like Psalm 34 and Romans 8:31-32. Every time another job opportunity would come up I would thank Him and believe that this was His provision for work; but it never materialised. I wondered if I was doing something wrong; why else would God be closing every door?

During this time God spoke to me. He reminded me of David and his journey to where God had called Him. In 1 Samuel 16, David is anointed as King over Israel. However, it was many years before he actually became King. The years in between, the years of waiting, the years between calling and Kingship, all brought David many hardships and it must have left him wondering if God really had called him to be King over Israel. Israel had many self-appointed and short-lived kings throughout history but it is David who is remembered above all. God was calling me to hold onto what He had called me to despite my current reality looking very different.

After a year of fruitless freelancing I decided to go to university. God had used the last year of disappointments to really humble me and shape my character. Without that past year I would never have thought that I needed to do a degree. I studied classical music, something I had no previous training in. It was the best thing that I could have done.

I spent the next three years soaking up everything around me. I dived into the incredible history of classical music and found some of the most amazing music. I learned how to write for the instruments of an orchestra. I had the opportunity to write music for dance, animations and documentaries and even to take modules from the jazz degree as part of my course. I graduated from university with a far greater depth of knowledge, experience and appreciation for music.

My assumption was that I would finish university, get a non-related job and hopefully increase my involvement in music-based work over the next couple of years but God had other plans.

Since finishing university a year ago He has provided me with work in the music industry. I have done a whole range of work including songwriting, orchestrating for film, collaborating for dance, teaching and composing on commission. The variety of work that I get to do is so beautiful. I get up every day thankful to God for the path He has taken me down (as painful as it might have been at times).

In fact, the journey that God has taken me on has led to a greater love for music. Since falling in love with music at the age of twelve, I have grown to love it more, the more I understand it. The music degree was a great example of this. I am increasingly giving glory to God every time He gives me new music to write or a new understanding of existing music. He truly is the great Musician.

This has been my first year that I have earned enough from music to pay tax. As small as it seems, it has taken me five years to get here so is a huge encouragement.

It has not been easy but I know I still need to trust in Him. It has been incredible to see God break me down over the years in order that my character would be changed to become more focused and reliant on Him.

Over the last year I have only ever had work for the month in front of me. I have no idea what kind of work I will be doing from month to month or even this time next year but that is part of the fun of trusting in God. It can still be a struggle when there is a dry spell, particularly given my past experience of not having work.

However, He is my Provider and He has and always will meet my needs.

Lightning Source UK Ltd.
Milton Keynes UK
UKHW012038300119
336485UK00010B/734/P